# A journey of Love

## A mother's memoir

## JENNIFER ALTHAUS

Cilento Publishing, Sydney, Australia
www.cilentopublishing.com

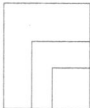

CILENTO
PUBLISHING

A central characteristic of someone with autism is a difficulty understanding and connecting with people; but that same person may have a natural ability to relate to animals. In return, animals seem to recognise the thoughts and feelings of those who have autism, and a genuine bond can develop between them. Dogs in particular often appear to have a 'sixth sense' in recognising distress in a person with autism, and a remarkable ability to calm and soothe someone if they are anxious and overwhelmed, unfortunately, a frequent emotional state for people on the autism spectrum.

This delightful story chronicles the loving connection between a severely anxious girl with autism and her dog. Where medication and conventional behaviour management strategies failed, this devoted greyhound succeeds in transforming her life.

Dr Tony Attwood is well known for sharing his knowledge of Aspergers Syndrome. He has an Honours degree in Psychology from the University of Hull, Masters degree in Clinical Psychology from the University of Surrey and a PhD from the University of London. He is currently adjunct Associate Professor at Griffith University in Queensland.

Tony has written several publications on Asperger's Syndrome. His book, titled Aspergers Syndrome, has now been translated into several languages.

www.tonyattwood.com.au

*For Celeste and Minnie....a team like no other.*

*For the parents, carers and loved ones of those with Autism. You are not alone. Together we unite in support, understanding, love and hope.*

*In memory of those Greyhounds who had their life cut short due to the terrors of the racing industry.*

# CONTENTS

# PROLOGUE

17 April 2015

If I could have one wish that would last a day it would be for a day full of happiness for Celeste. A day in which she felt good about herself, her anxiety allayed, smiling all day. Each day for my girl is a day of ups and downs. Happy and sharing to screaming and abusing and back again. I never know what to expect from one moment to another. Today we bought shoes which caused anxiety, but thankfully only minor meltdowns at the shop. These meltdowns happened when she wanted to put the shoes on. We purchased clothes for her and myself, again minor meltdowns but we dealt with them. We had a beautiful lunch together, talking about and sharing her clothes purchases keeping her happy.

It all happened when we got home. From 4pm until she eventually went to sleep at 10pm it was down hill. Screaming, calling me names, abusing the animals, thumping walls, throwing things. Why? Everything and anything was too hard. According to her the world was against her. She was on sensory overload from the stimulations of the day. Her mind was trying to absorb and make sense of her day. Too many new things, too many wants, too much everything. The more I tried to bring her down, to calm her, to talk to her, the more she abused me, cried and screamed. Leave her and she throws herself at me with abuse. It is a no win situation.

Overall I am tired, stressed and feel sad. To watch your child live like this, to have to live with this, is heartbreaking. What does the future hold for my baby?

# OUR WORLD OF AUTISM

Having a child with Autism is something no parent anticipates. Although my son, Alex, had been diagnosed as autistic, I did not expect the same fate for my daughter.

Autism (ASD) can be defined as a mental condition, present from early childhood, characterized by great difficulty in communicating and forming relationships with other people, and in using language and abstract concepts. The definitions and understanding of Autism varies from one person to another and one professional to another but what we can all agree on is that it is a debilitating disorder that controls the ability to understand social cues, language and to function within society in the way seen as the norm. No two people with Autism are the same, with the degree and difficulties varying from person to person. In the Autism community there is the well known saying, " If you've met one person with Autism, you've only met one person."

Celeste came into this world induced two weeks early due to gestational diabetes. She was eager to meet us, taking no time to show her presence once the induction started. From there on it was a different story. She was sluggish and really didn't care for the world. She struggled to suckle, suffering daily from severe reflux which medication seemed to alleviate only for very short periods. This lead to her gasping for breath with scary episodes of blueness. Sleeping upright on my chest became the norm. Today I question if these episodes were severe anxiety attacks present from birth.

As Celeste got older the gasping attacks got scarier. Gaining mobility only gave the attacks more power. When crawling or walking she would frequently stop to gasp, with episodes often lasting a minute or two. I remember clearly one episode where I thought we were going to lose her. The family was gathered around the table when Celeste instantly went blue in the face. No gasping, no warning. At the time she was sitting on my lap with nothing in her hands so I was sure she could not have put anything in her mouth. As the blueness covered her face her body became rigid and she started to throw herself forward as if having a convulsion. This lasted one to two very scary minutes until she eventually took a deep breath and sighed. With a rolling of her eyes her breathing, although laboured, returned to normal rhythm. Not long after this episode she fell asleep in my arms. A few weeks after this attack an echocardiogram was done on her heart but all was found to be normal. No reason or explanation medically or physically has ever been given for this attack. Celeste continued to have these gasping attacks on a regular basis until around the age of three. These lessened as the headbanging and self-harming became worse.

At the age of eighteen months I was sure the terrible twos had started early. The tantrums began as I had never seen before. I can't remember the head banging or banging of walls and doors at this age but I do remember episodes of her throwing herself on the floor, kicking and screaming as if there was no tomorrow. There were other things that rang alarm bells that I cannot put my finger on today. Maybe it was the vagueness in her eyes or the way she carried her body. Whatever it was things did not add up. I had been this road before, with Alex being diagnosed at the age of six, after a long battle with professionals in three different states of Australia. Any mother with a child with Autism will relate to stories of visits to one medical professional after another to be told it is behaviour management or your child just does not fit the criteria for Autism. They leave you wondering if you are a neurotic parent and make you question if you are going mad. You spend night after night crying, wondering what is wrong with your baby and wishing someone would just listen. Six used to be the magical age that children seemed to be diagnosed. Thankfully today, with advances in our knowledge of Autism, diagnosis and help is being offered much earlier.

Although I knew something was not right with Celeste I continued to live in denial. I was nowhere near ready to go through the diagnosis hell I went through with Alex. Surely I was imagining things, just worrying about nothing. As Celeste got older the tantrums, or shall we now call them meltdowns, got worse. She became violent towards herself, banging her head and chin, and also violent towards others, throwing things at people, including furniture. To take her out anywhere was a nightmare. Getting her dressed to leave, getting her in the car and then battling her while you were out was an exhausting and depressing task. Going out was soon something we only did when we really needed to. Not only was I feeling exhausted but her brother and sister could no longer cope. Everyone was at boiling point. She woke early and refused to sleep at night, waking most nights screaming with night tremors that lasted at least half an hour with me being unable to wake her. Each night I was terrified she would harm herself as she threw her little body around the bed screaming in rage at whatever was in her head. From the moment she woke to the moment she went to sleep I would battle with her over everything. The daily tasks we take for granted caused anxiety and tears. Playing with toys caused a meltdown. Even watching TV was too much for my poor little girl to handle.

The year Celeste turned six my eldest daughter, my rock and support, moved interstate to live with her boyfriend. For a while I crumbled feeling I had lost more than a daughter, I had lost someone who understood and supported me. Someone who had seen it, lived it and knew that what I experienced was real. I was now a single mum living with two children with Autism. I was living in Queensland with no family or close friends. I was lonely and scared. I felt as though my world was falling apart as each day I battled a six year old who I did not understand. I was at a loss as to what was going on. I knew it was Autism but I did not understand. Does a parent ever understand their autistic child? Oh, what we would do to get into their mind, if only for one day.

I was deeply involved in this. I had one child struggling with depression, for which he was now medicated, and who had developed Agoraphobia to complicate his lack of understanding of the world. Therapy was happening but his life wasn't. On the other end of the scale I had a raging bull, for want of a better way to describe her, who threw herself, verbally and physically at everything and everyone. Doors were slammed, walls were thumped, chairs were thrown and toys broken. If it was not bolted down it was not safe. Still today I cannot work out how one petite girl can find so much strength. Celeste cried and she hurt. Each day I watched the confusion and pain on her face. I saw the sadness in her eyes and, as she got older, I heard the "I'm sorry mum I love you" after she had raged at me. As her mother all I wanted was to take that pain away. She did not mean what she said, she did not want to hurt others. She was on sensory overload and did not know how to cope. For Celeste the world is a confusing place and the only way she knows how to cope is to fight back.

About a year after moving to Queensland I found an amazing doctor to whom I will forever be in debt. Dr Chambers changed my life. He listened to what I was saying; he spoke to Alex and understood and he was gentle with Celeste. Most of all he made me feel human. He understood where I was coming from as a mother and he wanted to help. Speech assessments and occupational therapy assessments were soon undertaken which confirmed what I was seeing. A trip to a paediatrician sent us backwards slightly as I was told, within less than two minutes of the paediatrician sighting Celeste, that there was nothing wrong with her. She was fine, just boisterous. To make matters worse this paediatrician was quick to tell me he had written about Autism and was regarded as an expert on the matter so knew Autism the minute it was presented to him. Considering no two Autistic people are the same I found this hard to grasp. According to him Celeste is verbal so she must be okay. Others who I spoke to about this doctor were dumbfounded.

My previous experiences with government paediatricians and Autism was reconfirmed. I am sure there are some good doctors in the government system but I have not yet found them.

Dr Chambers was there for me yet again. He listened and he encouraged me to push on. Next step was a referral to a psychiatrist, as in Queensland they too could diagnose. Dr Shah was my next knight in shining armour. On the day we saw him both children had appointments. Alex was struggling and the current counseling he was having was not helping. Dr Shah was not only on the ball with Alex, listening carefully to him, but took one look at Celeste, spoke to her for a while, asked relevant history, read her previous specialist reports and had no doubt about what we were dealing with. Next step was a visit to an occupational therapist for testing, along with clinical observation.

On 20th October 2014, after a lot of talking, testing and support I was handed the formal diagnosis of Autism Spectrum Disorder (ASD) with associated Anxiety. Celeste was seven years and five months. I was divided about how I felt. A sense of relief overcame me as I realised we would finally get the help we needed, but my heart felt heavy as the diagnosis confirmed my little girl's struggles, which were at a higher level than those I experienced with my son.

At the time Celeste was enrolled in Brisbane School of Distance Education in grade two but was only working at prep level. She was not reading, writing or understanding numbers. No matter what we did achievement was slow, if at all. With testing we were now starting to get an insight into some of the difficulties she had. She presented with a number of difficulties in the areas of social interaction and social communication. She presented with restricted and repetitive behaviour, speech and language delays, motor difficulties, cognitive difficulties, sensory processing difficulties and issues with emotional regulation. These difficulties were impacting on her ability to engage and interact with her environment. An auditory processing assessment, done in January of the following year, would show results that were consistent with a spatial awareness deficit, poor working memory and poor auditory skills. Severe headaches had also become a normal part of life which seems to be related to her anxiety.

With Celeste not progressing academically, she was enrolled in a special needs class within Brisbane Distance Education. The decision to take her from a normal class to one for special needs was made due to the fact that she was falling behind her peers at a rapid pace. Her teacher was a wonderful lady who took the time to adjust the curriculum as much as she could so that it met Celeste's needs but no matter what she did advancement was not being achieved.

By placing Celeste in a special needs class there was no pressure for her to meet the requirements of the curriculum. This meant Celeste could work at her own pace in the areas she needed. All subjects except English and Maths were dropped. Leaving Celeste with only two major subjects allowed us to focus on her ability. Even though this was possible by mid year we were still losing her as far as advancement in any areas of her education were concerned. Getting her to online classes each day was a nightmare. She would scream, throw the chair and lash out. Most days she would run away and hide. We tried everything but even rewards of her favourite things did not work. Completing worksheets that were required to be returned to the school as part of her assessment was a disaster. Again she would run away, all she wanted to do was run. Worksheets caused confusion in her mind. They challenged her to achieve, escalating her level of anxiety. Life is difficult enough for Celeste without having to process the information on a worksheet. Children with Autism do not see the world as others do. The Australian curriculum moves quickly, not allowing for those who need extra time and space to absorb nor does it take into consideration the obsessions and interest focus of a child with Autism. A meeting with the head of the special needs department was soon called and home educating was strongly suggested.

Our home educating journey began the following week. This was a journey I was comfortable with having taken it with Celeste the first year of her schooling life and with my other children previously, but I felt frustrated as I was back where I had started. I had enrolled Celeste in Brisbane School of Distance Education for support and help with her learning difficulties. It was my belief that the Department of Education was armed with the resources that were needed to assist children like Celeste but I was completely wrong.

There was one thing that gave me the confidence to move forward into a future of home educating, the fact that it had been endorsed by people within the government department who were meant to know what was best for our children as far as education was concerned. The home education application papers were completed and we were on our way to learning.

Home educating Celeste allows me to work with her at her own pace, working with her instead of against her. With more work and computer based learning Celeste is not focussed on the outcome but instead the enjoyment. Learning is no longer a chore but a natural and fun progression. By home educating we have been able to take away at least one of the factors in life that was causing her a high degree of anxiety. The anxiety is still there, although with the diagnosis came a trial of medications until Risperidone was administered and we saw a small amount of success. With medication the down time at night and sleep was achieved most nights, removing the tiredness which contributes to the inability to cope. With Autism it is a constant battle. Just when you think you have pieced it all together and life's a little smoother something, you never really know what, sends it all haywire again.

For Celeste day to day life will always be confusing and frustrating but as we continue to provide her with the therapy she needs to give her life skills and understanding of the world we can hope to lessen the confusion and help her find herself. At the moment she does not understand the world as a normal child does, with sounds, smells and social cues causing confusion that leads to violent meltdowns. She finds it difficult to do the simple things that children her age do such as going to the shops, visiting the cinema or museum. For Celeste daily tasks such as brushing her hair, bathing and getting dressed cause meltdowns.

At the age of seven she was still riding in a pram when out and about. This not only gave her a place of her own away from the overstimulation of people and noise but helped keep her, and those around her, safe when a meltdown occurred. She had become too big for a normal pram so I spent hours searching the internet for an alternative. E-Bay was eventually my answer as I came across a reasonably priced bike buggy that, when not hooked on the back of a pushbike, converted to a pram. By simply attaching a front wheel you had a pram that was fully enclosed with mesh windows. It had seats for two so there was plenty of room for Celeste and the menagerie of teddies and toys she just had to take with her when she walked out the door. With her headphones on to block out the noise, a blanket for sensory comfort and the cover fully enclosing her she was ready to conquer the world as best she could.

The disadvantage of this pram was size. I had a large 8 seater van but it still took up half the van when the back seats were folded up. There was little room for groceries. It was heavy to lift in and out of the car and difficult to unfold and fold up. The double width made it impossible to go into most shops and you definitely couldn't take it to crowded venues which was where it was needed most. I was excited to have a solution that, to a degree worked, but, like all parents, wanted the best for my child. Isolating her from the world when out was not a permanent solution. She was not learning to cope; instead she was learning to hide. She was limiting her ability to learn from the world around her.

It was whilst searching for a better solution that I came across Smart Pups and the use of assistant dogs as therapy for children with Autism. My world, and Celeste's, was about to change.

# LET THE JOURNEY BEGIN!

Our Smart Pups journey started late one night when my head was aching and my emotions were all over the place. I was ecstatic that I had finally got some answers to Celeste's meltdowns and that we were on the right path, but I was exhausted as there was no end to the battle each day. To say I was desperate was probably an understatement. I think only parents with children with disabilities or illness truly understand the level of desperation that is involved. One of the hardest things for any parent is to see their child battling or hurting on a day to day basis. Some would argue that a child with Autism is incapable of experiencing pain but those of us who see and live with an autistic child understand that this is not so.

To watch the confusion and sadness that overcomes your child, to hear your child apologize for what they have done with the pain evident in their voice, yet do the same thing again at the blink of an eye, causes emotional pain to both child and parent. It is as hard to explain as it is to understand but a child with Autism is not in control of their actions. They are instead controlled by the overload of the senses, be it touch, smell, sight or hearing, that is causing confusion within their mind. Imagine an annoying piercing noise that invades your ear space for hours on end. Eventually you are going to get headaches, feel stressed, anxious and angry. Not being able to escape would lead to pressure that would soon test your limits. Add to this the instructions and conversation of those who love you and you can understand why a meltdown eventually happens. Seeing my child live like this is what drove me to find something, anything that would assist my daughter in her daily struggle with life.

Animals have always been a part of our family. This was one of the driving forces behind my initial internet search on animals as therapy for children. We already had a Labrador x Kelpie named Beauty who had been in Celeste's life from the day she was born. As soon as Celeste started moving around Beauty was climbed on, cuddled and seen as a constant companion. Beauty is a maternal, loving dog who, never having had puppies of her own, saw Celeste as her responsibility from the day she came home from hospital. When Celeste started walking you could guarantee that wherever she was Beauty was there too. As Celeste grew so did the bond between her and Beauty. They had tea parties together, dress ups, dug in the sandpit, threw a ball and ran a mile together. Celeste loves to run. For her it is relaxation that slows her brain. When we were out and she had a meltdown I could be guaranteed that finding a place where she could run around in a circle would bring her back to me. In the beginning Beauty thought it was great but as the years passed and Beauty's age saw the onset of arthritis, the running became too much. The anxiety of Beauty not running often led to a meltdown. Eventually Celeste simply had to run by herself as Beauty sat and watched.

Beauty isn't the only therapy animal that Celeste has had in her life. There are her three Guinea Pigs: Peanut Butter, Licorice and Marshmallow. Marshmallow is actually Marshmallow two but we won't talk about the accidental death of Marshmallow one and the lesson that was learnt, and the week of meltdowns that followed.

Peanut Butter and Marshmallow were the first Guinea Pigs to come into Celeste's life. I had no idea when I agreed to Guinea Pigs how magical they would be. As a child I can remember having Guinea Pigs and my other two children had them, but they were not something I thought Celeste would handle. How wrong I was. Day after day she loved her Peanut Butter. She taught her tricks. We made outfits for her and she took her for walks in the pram. Peanut Butter soon got to know Celeste was Mum and would jump into her arms when she saw her. She would nestle in under Celeste's chin and look up at her lovingly. I have never seen anything like it. With the death of Marshmallow one and a time span where Celeste had shown she could be responsible with Peanut Butter, Licorice was added to the family. Licorice was a long haired black Guinea Pig who soon won my heart. A year or two passed and with the death of one of my mum's Guinea Pigs we soon inherited her other Guinea Pig who Celeste insisted on naming Marshmallow two, in memory of her long lost friend. Although Celeste could not run with her Guinea Pigs they showed her love and revealed the potential of therapy on a whole new level. When the TV was on you could guarantee a Guinea Pig was being stroked and that a level of calmness, that would not normally be seen in Celeste, was present. When she was coming down from a meltdown a cuddle and pat with a Guinea Pig was often the therapy that worked. When she needed someone to listen there was always a Guinea Pig willing to sit quietly without judgement.

Celeste's seventh birthday saw the adoption of two pet rats, Rufus and Charlie. Again I was skeptical. She was adamant that she wanted a pet rat for her birthday. Being sure that the rat would be left in the cage and ignored, I insisted we get two so that they had company. I need not have worried. Rufus and Charlie soon became as loved and handled as our other pets. Every morning Celeste would get them out and let them run around on the bathroom floor where they were safe. She kissed them numerous times each day and handled them. She spoke to them gently and lovingly and tried as hard as she could to teach them tricks. She loved 'her babies' to the extent that one could say was a bit obsessive. They were even dressed as Batman and Robin for a country show and entered in the best dressed pet category. Have you ever tried to make an outfit for a rat? Believe me it is not an easy task, especially when a child with anxiety, who has her mind set on one thing, is involved. Rufus and Charlie didn't win the best dressed but they did win second prize in the most unusual pet section receiving one dollar and a certificate for their effort. The biggest winner was myself as I witnessed a grin from ear to ear on Celeste's face. It is the small things in life that matter. The smiles and the memories are priceless.

So one may wonder why I would even consider adding another pet to the family. Did I mention we also have two cats who are therapy for Alex, and three goldfish which just do what goldfish do best, swim. Each pet we have gained has been shown only to enrich Celeste's, and the family's, life. They all serve their role. They calm Celeste in many different ways, teach her different responsibilities, different social skills and communicate with her in different ways. Although now getting on in her years, Beauty is still the one Celeste plays roughly with, sits on, lies with and gives unlimited cuddles. The Guinea Pigs are the real life dolls, the ones willing to be dressed up and to sit in the doll's pram and be pushed around, the ones that will sit still for a brush or a stroke with the hand when calm is needed in a close and small way. The rats are Celeste's babies, who we sadly said goodbye to due to death, Charlie to illness and Rufus twelve months later to old age. They showed her unconditional love in only a way a rat can. She could pick them up in her hand

and place them against her cheek and stroke them. She could give them an oh so gentle kiss. They brightened her day as they ran around the floor and explored. Rats pooping on the floor is ever so funny to a young child.

The one thing that all of Celeste's pets cannot do is provide her with the comfort, support and assistance needed when she is outside of the confines of her own home. This is a time that anxiety and overload is its highest. A time of uncertainty and sensory overstimulation. A time when a meltdown is not only inappropriate and stressful for all around her but also dangerous. It is for this reason that an assistance dog was of high interest to myself. Maybe, just maybe, an assistance dog would make the world outside of the safe confines of her home a little bit easier for Celeste. Over time, just maybe, we could grab some groceries without a meltdown, a struggle or a headache. Maybe just once I could manage to collect all the groceries I needed instead of abandoning half of them behind as I leave in a hurry. This of course leads to more trips to the shops to grab what is needed which leads to more meltdowns. A never ending rollercoaster. Maybe one day Celeste would have the opportunity to attend museums and events and learn hands on about her world. Maybe one day she could attend a theme park and laugh like the other kids instead of screaming. Maybe just maybe...

Finding the Smart Pups internet page was an accident that was magical. My instant reaction when I opened the page was, 'Oh My God!' My heart and stomach signalled that this was it...it then all deflated. $20,000! Each family must raise $20,000 to be eligible for a Smart Pup, and that was only after you had filled out the application form and been accepted. What were my chances? Could I ever raise that amount of money if my application was successful? What if it didn't work? And so the doubtful questions snuck into my mind. But my gut instinct took hold and I knew, just knew in my heart that this was it. I had to give it a go.

I kept reading the Smart Pups web page and focusing on the positive. As I read words such as 'Smart Pups Autism Assistance dogs can dramatically enhance the quality of life for a child with Autism' and 'Children have a special connection with animals, particularly dogs, and a child with Autism can gain a sense of safety, calmness and understanding through their bond with a Smart Pup.' My heart fluttered with hope. We already knew of the bond between Celeste and animals. As I read on I felt more and more confident that I had found what my daughter needed: 'Having a trusty Smart Pup companion at their side increases an autistic child's ability to cope with life, helps ease sensory overload and provides emotional support. A Smart Pup acts as a bridge between the child and the outside world. Its role is to guide the child through their daily routine, keep them safe and comfort them when the world just gets too much.'

I had to give it a go. What did I have to lose. The first step was to submit an application. I was sure there would be a long waiting list and our application might not even be successful. I can't remember what the time frame was between viewing the site and sending off the application but I am sure it was only a matter of days, if not hours. I remember the application being one that was rather easy and submitting was only a matter of sending the application via email. I do remember that once I submitted my application it was a while before I even got acknowledgment that my application had been received. I spent days worrying that it had not arrived. I was also sure that this meant they got hundreds, if not thousands of applications a day. On 2nd September 2014 I received an email from Smart Pups advising me that my application had been received and would be processed at the end of the month. It was irrelevant to Smart Pups at this time that Celeste was yet to have a formal diagnosis for Autism but this worried me as I felt it would surely mean we would miss out on our chance of success. Maybe my desperation for help had caused me to jump the gun a little. Maybe I should have waited till the diagnosis was formal. With this worrying me I emailed Smart Pups on 11th September informing them that both children had seen Dr Shah on the 9th September and that although we still had to undergo further testing, Dr Shah felt certain Celeste fit the criteria for Autism. The testing was to take place on 7th October. To my delight I received a reply of reassurance thanking me for the update, stating it would be added to my file. I breathed a sigh of relief, feeling a little better about our chances of success.

The time from this letter to our successful application seemed to drag. Not being sure of how I would be notified I watched my inbox, eagerly awaited the mail each day and my heart skipped a beat each time the phone rang hoping it may be a positive phone call. Having not heard anything, and being eight days past our official diagnosis, I sent Smart Pups another update message on 28th October. The purpose of my email was two-fold. Firstly I felt it important that I let them know our diagnosis was official but I was also anxious to know if we had a date we could expect to get an answer from them. I was excited to receive a reply stating Celeste was on the list for the October round of applications which they hoped to process the following day, getting back to people on the Friday or Saturday of that week. After taking a deep breath, and a moment to gather my thoughts, I crossed everything I had and waited.

On 31 October 2014 I received the news I so badly wanted to hear. 'I am pleased to advise that your application to Smart Pup for an Autism Assistance Dog for your daughter, Celeste, has been successful and am delighted to be able to offer you a place on the Smart Pups Program. Attached to this email was a letter of offer, information sheet and the terms and conditions of placement. I was to notify them of my intention to proceed or withdraw from the program.

Withdraw! Are they kidding me!

Like the Autism diagnosis the successful application left me elated and full of hope yet scared and worried about raising so much money. Focusing on the positive I rang family members to tell them the news. They all congratulated me on my successful application but were divided in their support. There were those who, although they did not have much to say, were positive and then there were those who focussed on the negative – you will never raise that much money; Celeste will only lash out at the dog; it won't work and all you will end up with is another dog to feed. Why is it that no one else is ever as excited about something as you are?

My life is built very much on ignoring the negative and embracing the positive and that was exactly what I did in this situation. I allowed the excitement and the hope to engulf me and I used the negative to empower me. I would show those naysayers and prove them wrong. I knew what was right for my little girl. I observed her behaviour towards her pets every day and something told me that this was what she needed. If I was wrong then, and only then, the negative people could say they told me so...but what if I was right?

Later that evening I emailed my intention to proceed to Smart Pups. On 11th November my intention was acknowledged and I received a letter of authority to fundraise on behalf of Smart Pups along with a fundraising kit full of ideas and encouragement.

So what do you do when you need to raise so much money? You put your heart and soul into it and you give it all you have. My first thoughts were to jump online and see what others were doing and what fundraising options I had. I spoke to anyone who would listen and gave those who wouldn't no choice but to listen. I sent email after email to local businesses, and anyone I thought might be interested. Naturally more went out than came back but with each response I got, with each kind – hearted reply, my hope grew.

I never really had a fundraising plan. I just allowed the love of my daughter and the desire for a better life for her to drive me. I started a Go Fund Me Crowdfunding page and I started spreading it far and wide using social media. As donations came in my hope rose. A dollar here and a dollar there all helped. I soon learnt though that crowdfunding is not for the light hearted. The setting up of the page alone takes a lot of thought. How do you sell your cause in a way that encourages complete strangers to hand over their hard earned cash? As I put my skills as a publicist to the test I came to realise that I had the ability to tackle these daunting tasks, abilities that many would never have. Grabbing hold of my determination and motherly love I wrote from the heart.

I soon learnt that it takes a lot of work and many hours of sharing and talking up your cause to make any money using crowdfunding. Like all things there definitely is no such thing as overnight success. One can jump online and read of those who raised thousands but what you do not see is the amount of time and effort that goes into these campaigns. As the months passed I was grateful for every cent but we were still a very long way from our target. Phase two of our fundraising campaign started. I jumped on Gumtree, an online sales site, and sold bits and pieces. With the help of some wonderful businesses who donated tickets, items and bits and pieces I was able to fundraise more and more. The tally grew but at this rate it was still going to take years, something my desperation for help for Celeste told me I did not have.

Phase three, that of selling Cadbury fundraising chocolate using social media, saw our tally grow a little more as family and friends spread the word. As orders came in via messenger and email, chocolates were packed into postage satchels and shipped out. Individuals bought in bulk and businesses took boxes off our hands selling them in their reception area.

As the fundraising was happening my life continued to fall apart. The one saving grace was that I had the fundraising to take my mind off the rages that Celeste had every moment of the day. I spoke to her about her acceptance for a Smart Pup, amusing her by showing her videos of assistance dogs and including her in the journey. I read her messages of hope that people sent us on Facebook and showed her our crowdfunding tally with each donation. In her own way Celeste understood what we were aiming for and in the beginning it made her smile but as time passed she lost interest, just as she does in all things around her. For me it was my timeline. It was the therapy I needed to keep going each day...my little ray of sunshine on a gloomy day. The least I could do was share it with my daughter and let her know I was trying to help.

I had good days and bad days. One of the positive things about fundraising is that no matter how you feel each day there is always someone there listening and wanting to help. On the bad days the smiles and compassion of others is what keeps you going. As a fundraiser you soon become part of a community. This community, one of people all aiming to meet a goal, understands and welcomes you. The members support each other when they can and open the door to those outside of the community to support them. They understand your struggle to spread the word, offering advice and ideas. Then there are the strangers who offer their donations, the ones who place a smile on your face, touch your heart and care. There are the anonymous who donate and you really never get to thank and then there are those who you chat with, exchanging words of warmth that often lead to long term friendships.

At the time of fundraising one of Celeste's obsessions was that of watching Mommy and Gracie on YouTube. She was totally addicted to this mother and daughter duo who review dolls and toys. Mommy and Gracie were the ones who started Celeste's craze with Monster High dolls. If Mommy and Gracie said it was awesome it must be. The personalities of this duo were infectious, with Celeste mimicking things Gracie said word for word, including the American accent. The more Celeste became obsessed with Mommy and Gracie the more she bugged me to send them an email and let them know she loved them. I can't remember exactly what I said within this email but do know that I mentioned our fundraiser. The following morning I received a beautiful reply from Melissa (Mommy) along with a donation to our crowdfunder. It touched my heart that a complete stranger could be so generous.

One of the biggest disappointments I found was the lack of support from large corporate groups. The larger the company the more they demanded from you before they offered to give not only support financially but their time. The saying that the more money one has the more one wants is so true. The more money they have the more bureaucracy becomes involved which of course brings with it fees that cut into your fundraising tally. Still today I scratch my head at how a medium size shopping centre in Ipswich Queensland can charge a fee of $80 for a fundraising 'booth' they hire to charities. This 'booth' is a small table-like set up with two chairs, propped outside the front of Woolworths. When hiring this 'booth' the charity must also produce documentation of their own public liability insurance. What happened to helping your fellow man and supporting charities who support others?

Of course there are exceptions to the rule when it comes to big corporations and to those, who take the time to listen and consider the little man, lending a hand, I say thank you. Movieworld, Australia Zoo and Events Cinemas are three corporations who offered a friendly smile and support during our fundraiser.

This was not the first time Movieworld had shown us kindness. On our first trip to Movieworld, which was prior to a Smart Pup coming into our lives, Celeste struggled. I would have to say it was one of the worst experiences of my life as far as Autism and the inability to cope went. As soon as we arrived the meltdowns began. The environment was way too overwhelming. She wanted to go home but she wanted to stay and enjoy the rides. The hands went over the ears and she clung to me.

She would stop every now and then throwing herself on the ground and curling up into a ball. At one stage we decided we would take a break and watch the Hollywood Stunt Drivers Show. A break it was not. What I had not thought of was the noise and smell of burning rubber that the show produced. I soon found myself heading toward the exit carrying a screaming child who was a complete mess. Thankfully the girl at the door saw me coming and assisted me with my exit. As soon as I got on the other side of the door Celeste threw herself on the ground, hands over ears and started rocking. All I could do was sit on the ground and cuddle her.

Batman became my hero. Celeste has always liked Batman but on this particular day he was our knight in shining armour. While Celeste tried to pull herself out of her meltdown Batman emerged and stood in front of the door to Gotham City, which was near where we were sitting. I seized the moment, drawing attention to him. To my delight Batman looked our way, seeming to make eye contact with Celeste. That was enough to pull her out of her slump and have her up and off to say hello. She joined the small cue to meet her hero. With a smile on her face, and confidence I had never seen, especially after a meltdown, she approached Batman and stood beside him. Getting down to her level Batman spent a moment with her. He showed her how to stand like he does, tough and ready to conquer the world and a photo was taken. Celeste left her hero with a spring in her feet, a tall upright body, a smile from ear to ear and ready to conquer the world. Our day had changed completely. She still had meltdowns waiting for a ride but at the mention of Batman she found new strength. The photo of her and Batman hangs on our wall as a reminder of the strength Batman holds.

Upon returning home I emailed customer service at Movieworld and told them of my experience, thanking them kindly for what was provided and asking them to personally thank the man who was Batman on that day. I received a beautiful reply from them in which they proceeded to organise free entry tickets and a personal meet and greet for the family with Batman. Celeste was beside herself. Our second visit to Movieworld went much more smoothly, with our meet and greet with Batman creating a special moment Celeste will never forget.

With crowdfunding taking up the majority of my time yet leaving me feeling it would be years before we were anywhere near our target, I decided to jump online and search for funding. It was worth a shot. I was a writer after all, surely I could tackle a funding application and I did, after all, have just as much chance as anyone else.

Google soon answered my prayers leading me to two organisation that we fit the criteria for, The Shane Warne

Foundation (Necessitous Circumstances Fund) and The Courier Mail Children's Fund. Soon after discovering The Shane Warne Foundation I read of a family who had received some of the funding from them for their Smart Pup. This gave me hope, which soon turned to confusion as the website told me that funding was open for the year yet the application form was for the year previous. A quick email soon sorted this out providing a link to the correct form, with the online form issue being rectified in the near future for other applicants.

The dinner table soon became a sea of papers as I printed the applications, gathered all the documentation needed and set about writing the best funding application I possibly could. With butterflies in my stomach and hope in my heart Celeste and I kissed both envelopes as we popped them into the post box. With application closing dates being a few months away the plan was to take a small break from fundraising, starting again in January of the next year.

With our funding applications posted we got on with life, trying hard to forget about them. Preparations for Christmas kept us busy along with Celeste attending occupational therapy, speech therapy and seeing a psychologist each week.

The new year saw us adding home educating as a new focus, with fundraising once again taking a high priority. Our goal was to make this year the year we raised funds for our Smart Pup. Together we watched our fundraising tally grow, discussing the numbers and money, adding each dollar. We read about assistance dogs and used animals as our interest to engage learning. It did not mean Celeste magically read or grasped the concept of numbers but what she did do was start to enjoy learning. Learning is only a task if it is made one. I have always home educated my children by the motto of 'Life is learning, learning is life'.

As an adult I am always studying a course of some sort or reading, showing my children that we are never too old to learn. When it came to learning for Celeste the basics of reading, writing and numbers were not of importance at this stage. Each day she struggled with simple life skills so it was only sensible that she learnt to cope with these without added pressure. If I could relieve some of the stresses of life, the anxiety and the sensory overload, then surely the rest would follow.

It was also at about this time that our world was turned upside down in a positive way.

# ACTS OF KINDNESS

Life became very busy very quickly. Not a day passed that I did not think of our submissions but I tried not to dwell on them. Still desperate and with six months having passed, which I now realise is not long as far as trying to raise $20,000, I was sure we would never make it. At this stage we had only raised just over $1,000. Celeste was not improving. Home educating was no miracle cure. The meltdowns escalated to the degree that I was not only concerned about holes in my walls but about Celeste harming herself. Each day I became more desperate. Tiredness set in as I went to bed exhausted and woke feeling no better. Celeste shared my bedroom and my bed. Each night she slept alongside me as her anxiety made it impossible for her to be in a room alone, day or night. This also meant that I would have to get into bed at the same time as her each night, lying there while she fell asleep, leaving when she was in a deep sleep, at the risk of her waking and the discovery of my absence leading to an anxiety attack. The meltdowns started at sunrise and didn't stop until Celeste was in a deep slumber. I had never dealt with this before as with Alex it had been the opposite. Sleeping all day being his way of coping with the world.

Celeste was placed on Melatonin to try to encourage a restful sleep but this was found to be of no use. Risperidone was our saviour, leading to lessening of the night tremors. Risperidone is a drug used for mental and mood disorders not only associated with autism but also prescribed for schizophrenia and bipolar disorder. It is classed as an atypical antipsychotic, helping to restore the balance to certain natural substances in the brain. Like all drugs there was the risk of some side effects such as increased appetite, nausea, weight gain and tiredness. With Celeste being a little soul with a poor appetite I felt that the weight gain and increased appetite probably would not be a problem. The other effects could be dealt with if they occurred. Celeste was started on a small dose in the hope that this not only meant she got a restful sleep but so did I. We hoped that with a good sleep the days would be smoother but this did not prove to be the case, although side effects have never been an issue. As time progressed we found it necessary to increase the dose of Risperidone.

Total exhaustion and discouragement soon lead me to feeling disheartened with our Smart Pup journey and looking for yet another solution. I was still convinced that an assistance dog was the answer but I needed a more proactive and quicker solution. Celeste and her connection to her pets reinforced this each day. Surely there was a cheaper way of achieving an assistance dog. Suddenly the light bulb in my mind lit with another brain wave, making me smile as I recalled Alex making a ding sound when he was younger every time he had a thought process. Baffled as to why he did this we finally realised he was replaying a cartoon he had seen in which a bell made a ding, ding noise and a light in a caption box came on above the dog's head each time he had a thought. As my light bulb dinged the idea of privately training an assistance dog came to my mind. Surely there was a way of doing this and surely it would mean I could pay as I trained, breaking our large goal down into small achievable goals. A quick search of dog trainers lead me to private trainers who were certified to do the job. The next question was where do I find a dog and what breed is best.

It is funny how things happen. One night I was casually scrolling Facebook when I came across a video that Todd McKenney, of Dancing with The Stars and theatre fame, had placed on his page. It was a segment from the Morning Show earlier that day where Todd introduced his Greyhounds and spoke of them as pets.

As I read the comments on the post I became excited. Everyone was speaking of the beautiful calming nature of the Grey, sharing photos of their fur babies. For some reason I casually jumped in on the conversation.

> *'I am seriously looking into adopting. I need a dog that will run with my eight year old daughter as she is active, but still also sit and keep her calm when she has meltdowns (she has Autism). She needs a companion dog. I work from home and my daughter is homeschooled so there is always someone home with the dog. Making more enquiries.'*

Not expecting Todd McKenney to answer, as after all celebrities are very busy people, I was surprised when he acknowledged my question with a simple, "Then these are the dogs for you."

This led to a day long thread of thirty five comments where people shared their experiences and photos. This had me searching Autism and Greyhounds, finding that they are great companion dogs who are used regularly overseas for those with Autism. I soon came across Dawn Joy-Leong and her beautiful Greyhound, Lucy, who are based in Sydney. Lucy attends university with Dawn each day as her assistance dog. Today Dawn and Lucy have become supportive friends of ours and although they have since moved back to Singapore, technology means support is not so far away. Dawn is an adult who had developed her own level of ability to cope and, studying a degree at university that was based around Autism, was very aware of her struggles and the techniques she needed to associate with the 'normies' of this world. With this in mind I wondered if a Greyhound would be suitable for a child who was still very much finding herself and her way in life.

My own stress and anxiety was easing. I had found a community of people who, although Autism was not a common factor, had the love of dogs in their blood which raised my spirits. They gave me hope, made me feel welcome and made me smile.

The support was so overwhelming that I felt a need to message Todd McKenney and thank him for allowing my comment to take over his Facebook post and for his kind words and support. I had previously messaged Todd about our fundraiser as something had compelled me to do so. Contacting celebrities is not something I would normally do but I felt a connection to Todd prior to the post. I was being led towards him and at the time I did not know why. Todd never responded to my message in regards to fundraising but, like all celebrities, he gets many of these. At the time I was not aware that my compulsion to contact Todd was for completely different reasons.

My Facebook message was meant to be one of thank you, not one of expecting a reply or support, but I got more than I expected for which I will be ever grateful.

> *'On 5th February I had a feeling to message you, above, about our fundraiser for an Autism Assistance Dog for my daughter Celeste. Little was I to know that our connection was actually you leading me to what my daughter really needs, a Greyhound companion. The more I researched and read about Greyhounds today and the more people I spoke to the*

*more I knew this was what was meant to happen. I will still need to raise money for the dog and training but I know this is what is going to happen and be life changing for my daughter and the Greyhound. Thank you so much for taking a moment to acknowledge my comment on your status and for your support. I will document our journey and keep you up to date. Have an absolutely awesome week. Huge thank you and hugs from me.'*

It was midnight when Todd replied.

*'No worries Jennifer. I've posted many things on FB but I've never seen a response to a person's reply like the one you have had regarding a companion pup for Celeste. It's quite heart warming. You'll need to find the right dog of course and that might be a trial and error situation. Greys are like every other breed and they each have their own personalities but in general Greys are pretty cool, calm and collected in most situations (unlike what we have just seen on 4 Corners). I'd like to help get the right dog for you and Celeste so if you would like to contact my manager on Monday and fill her in on your situation she will hook us up for a chat on the phone and we can take things from there. One thing you do need to know is Greys are really hard to train. Even getting them to sit is difficult but I still think they are worth a try. Thanks, Todd.'*

I now read Todd's comment on Greys being hard to train and to teach to sit and have to smile as this is so not what we have experienced today, but at the time, this was the general message I was getting from many.

The relationship between Todd, myself, Celeste and our future Greyhound had been set in concrete.

That night was a busy night of chatting as Dawn responded to a message I sent her. Emails back and forth were made with Dawn offering support and providing me with a life-line into the mind of someone who has to live with Autism.

It is amazing how the kind words and support of complete strangers can change your mood and make life seem a little easier. That night I slept peacefully. The next day was no different to any other as far as living with Autism was concerned but the activity of the night before had instilled that little bit of hope of a brighter future. Hope that drove me to continue to go forward.

As Monday greeted us with warmth and sunshine I made contact with Todd McKenney's manager, a beautiful lady who, although she was not sure what was going on, made me feel welcome. Her friendly disposition and willingness to listen gladdened my heart.

It was not long after contact with his manager that Todd rang me and the plan to find the ideal Greyhound for the job was put into place. Todd asked me all the right questions that allowed him to get a feel for our requirements and shared with me the love he had for his Greys. We briefly discussed the issues within the racing industry at the time and our passion to make changes to the lives of Greys. At no time was Todd judgmental or opinionated about the industry but was a true gentleman who spoke words of kindness. Our conversation soon lead to the different Greyhound adoption organisations that are available in New South Wales and Queensland and to the Greys that I had found online over the weekend. When discussing the other animals in my household we agreed that consideration would need to be given to finding a Grey that was cat friendly so as to not cause conflict between Celeste's beloved pets.

The hunt for our Greyhound had started. I wrote an overview paper of the situation which I emailed to Todd who then set about showing it to Greyhound adoption places in New South Wales. While Todd handled New South Wales I tackled Queensland. Calls and emails between Todd and myself flowed as we kept each other up to date on what was happening each end. New South Wales Greyhound Racing stated they did not have a dog that was suitable at that current moment and when contacting their Queensland branch did not feel they had one either but they would keep us in mind.

The biggest problem we were finding was that of the cats. With each adoption organisation I contacted I became more disheartened as most were not overly friendly. When I explained what I was seeking, they all stated that finding a Grey who was cat friendly was the real challenge. I feel the unfriendliness really came from the fact that I was seeking a Greyhound to be used as an assistance dog. When this was mentioned, which was always early in the conversation, the tone and way they dealt with me changed. Maybe the concept was too new for them or maybe it was that the assistance required was for a child, giving them the misconception that the dog would be at risk of harm. There were two particular organisations in Queensland who I found to be particularly negative, and who shall remain anonymous, but they both gave me the impression that my idea of a Greyhound as an assistance dog was totally ridiculous, laughable even. The attitude of 'You can't teach a Grey to sit' and 'A Grey will never come when you call it,' continued.

There is a light at the end of every tunnel and as you walk towards it you collect an abundance of positivity that pushes all the negativity aside. This was evident during this journey. As I rang Greyhound adoption places in Queensland and the negativity hit me I watched the media and internet outrage concerning the current baiting scandal within the Greyhound industry. I found it hard to understand why the adoption places were not falling over backwards to help me but were instead telling me I would never find the right dog. Surely the number of dogs put up for adoption was only going to rise, now was not the time to be discouraging someone who was interested in giving a Greyhound a new life.

As program after program discussed the baiting scandal that had been uncovered by Four Corners I followed the posts on Facebook, commenting whenever I could. With each comment I posted, mentioning my seeking a Grey, I was rewarded with an abundance of positive comments. I remember one post in particular. The Greyhound Equality Society shared a segment that The Project had aired. My comment wasn't anything out of the ordinary. I spoke of how depressed I felt about the current baiting situation and that I was willing to give a Grey a home but was feeling discouraged by the messages I was getting from the adoption industry in regards to cats. Before I knew it the comment was bombarded with reply after reply of positivity. The kindness of others yet again reached out to me, sharing photos of their Grey's snuggled up to cats. Not only were there cats but there were chickens, rabbits and a variety of animals one would be cautioned against placing with a Grey. The kind words and the links to places to go to look for a Grey touched my heart.

Whilst I was caught up in the news and Facebook chat I was forgetting about one Greyhound adoption place who had not yet responded to my email contact. This organisation was Greyhounds New Beginnings. Situated in Queensland they are a small not for profit organisation run by two lovely ladies, Buffy and Sarah, and a mountain of volunteers.

While out shopping one day I missed the call that was to be the start of changes in our life. That was the call from Sarah, a call in response to my email pleading my case and asking her if they had a suitable Grey. I can't remember who eventually rang whom back but have a feeling I rang Sarah and left her a message and then she eventually got me. What I do remember was answering the phone and hearing the voice of an angel, the voice of someone with whom I instantly connected, someone who listened. I was sure the call would only lead to being told ' Sorry I can't help you; your cats are an issue and a Grey will never sit', but instead I got a positive response and a woman who really wanted to help. Sarah came across as being someone who knew Greyhounds well, asked all the right questions about my situation and said 'yes'. I remember the word 'yes' as if it was yesterday. It was music to my ears. Yes, we would love to help you. Yes, we will do our best to find you a suitable Grey and Yes! You can have Greys and cats in the same household. Yes, yes, yes.....

Sarah spoke of two Greyhounds she had that she felt might be suitable. She asked for twenty-four hours to think about which dog would be more suitable for each of the two homes wanting dogs because, although Minnie was scheduled to go to other owners, she felt she may be perfect for Celeste.

On the same day I had the conversation with Sarah I got a phone call from The Courier Mail Children's Fund. When I answered the phone and the lady introduced herself I was expecting further questions to assist our application. She casually asked me how our fundraising was going before saying we could stop fundraising as our funding had been successful and The Courier Mail were going to give us the full $20,000. To say I was speechless is an understatement. The poor lady was left sitting on the other end of a silent line as I gathered myself together. I just wanted to cry. This was much better than winning the lottery. I vaguely remember asking her if she was joking. Her comment was to state that my speechlessness had actually made her day. She said that there were others in the office who were commenting that my reaction was what they love about their job. Still today I would love to meet this office full of wonderful people and give them a hug. Still today I pinch myself as nothing as good as this had ever happened to me and I am sure nothing will ever beat it. After hanging up and picking myself up off the floor I set about ringing and texting everyone I knew to share my amazing news, pinching myself regularly while the back of my mind still questioned whether it was a prank call.

That night I wrote on Facebook:

> Today has shown me how quickly things can change. This afternoon I have had a one in a million phone call that has left me speechless. I was touched by the events of last year but this year is going to exceed them. Today has strengthened my belief that if you put the message out into the universe and keep striving toward your goal your message will be answered. Keep believing! Keep dreaming!

I did not announce the approval of funding to the world on that particular night. The next day I took Celeste out for a celebration lunch. It was then, using photos of Celeste at lunch that I announced that funding had come through. The response was heartwarming.

I was now faced with a dilemma. I had the $20,000 needed for a Smart Pup but it also looked as though I may have found a Greyhound. My mind raced. Accepting the $20,000 gave us our dog but I was aware that the wait with

Smart Pups once you had raised your money could be twelve months or more. At the time I questioned if I could make it through another twelve months of being isolated at home due to meltdowns and socially unacceptable behaviour when out. The training process of each Smart Pup was lengthy and not all passed the grade. If I went with the option of training a Grey I may have the help Celeste needed more quickly but this may also fail.

Naturally the Smart Pup road was the easiest for me as it meant I would not have to face the headache of training. Could I hold out for another twelve months knowing that the help was close but not close enough? Would training our own dog be any quicker? Not being one to stress over decisions for too long I decided to be greedy and go with both. After all I did not even know if the Greyhound Sarah had for us was going to be suitable for our family. The worst that could happen is that we would add a new member to our family and that was something we could all surely live with.

The next day was Friday the 13th, a day some would say is unlucky, but for us it bought all the luck we could ever have dreamed of. Sarah rang me back as promised with the news that she had spoken to the people who were going to take Minnie and discussed the situation with them. She was sure Minnie was best for us and that the other people were fine with trial running the other dog. Minnie was ours. When would we like to pick her up?

Two days later Celeste, Alex and me were on our way to pick up our girl. I remember the drive to pick Minnie up as though it was yesterday. I was excited yet nervous. This journey surely was a roller coaster of emotions. It was arranged that we would foster Minnie in the first instance, giving us a chance to assess if she was not only the right dog for our family but had the right temperament for the job of an assistance dog.

It was a 40 minute drive to Sarah's where we would be collecting Minnie. The conversation all the way there was about our new friend. We knew she was black and that her name was Minnie but that was all we knew. How big was she? What did Greyhounds eat? Where would she sleep? How would Beauty react to having a new dog in the house? Sarah had asked if we could bring Beauty with us as she would love to meet her, so Beauty had come along with us for the drive. I wasn't worried about how Celeste would react to Minnie as I knew how she was with dogs but I was concerned she would have a meltdown at Sarah's house. Little did I know that it would not be Celeste who embarrassed me but Beauty, who disgraced herself, and the family by defecating on Sarah's floor. Not only did it stink but she managed to find the rug instead of the floorboards. I was most apologetic but Sarah, being use to new dogs gracing her lounge room, took it all in her stride.

When we arrived at Sarah's it was a little overwhelming so I could not say we formed any opinion of Minnie. There was a small collection of Greys and other dogs to attend to along with dealing with Beauty. Papers were filled out and we were armed with all we needed to make Minnie feel comfortable while we were fostering her. As a foster carer for Greyhounds New Beginnings you are provided with a metal framed dog bed, muzzle (as some councils in Queensland, and other states, still require the muzzling of Greys when in public), a few weeks' supply of food and a winter coat.

We were soon in the car and on our way home. It was here that my heart skipped a beat as I looked in the rear view mirror. There was Minnie sitting on the car seat beside Celeste with her head on Celeste's lap. Celeste was quietly stroking her. Alex quickly snapped a photo. The love in the eyes of both of them was priceless. I knew in that moment that Minnie was the right dog for us.

That night I wrote the following diary notes: ...

> *What an adorable dog she is. She instantly took to the whole family, sitting nicely in the car on the trip home. She has bonded instantly with Beauty. She is very cuddly, instantly taking to the queen bed. The lounge was also soon taken over.*

My Facebook post of the night was Minnie sleeping peacefully with her head on a pillow and a blanket over her. From day one Celeste has made sure her girl is comfortable at all times.

You often hear of people saying a dog chose them, or a dog came into their life just at the right time. I am positive that from the moment we placed Minnie in the car she knew why she was coming to live with us and what her role was to be. The bonding with Celeste was instant. Some things are surely meant to be...

With Minnie now in our life and already showing that she should stay I was back to facing the dilemma of self training versus Smart Pups, initial bonding with the chance of failure versus waiting and then forming a new bond. While I was making my decisions the Australian Government was left with bigger decisions as the outcry from society in regards to the live baiting scandal became louder and louder. The future for Greyhound racing in Australia and the future of the Greys within the industry hung in the balance.

# THE FUTURE OF GREYHOUNDS...

With Minnie came not only hope for my family but hope for Greyhounds as a breed. We had found our Greyhound at the time of the turmoil within the industry and I was sure that the success of Minnie as an assistance dog could be used to help create awareness of the ability of Greyhounds and encourage adoption.

ABC Four Corners, a national Australian show that had been exposing scandals, triggering inquiries and causing debate since 1961, was at its best. The exposure of live baiting within the Greyhound racing industry, in their documentary titled 'Making a Killing' (February 16, 2015) spread around the globe, causing the Greyhound Racing industry to face fallout within Australia. This industry, that was already often under fire, was now plunged into the depth of public attention.

Footage showing live piglets, possums and rabbits being dragged around the track by a mechanical lure as they were chased by Greyhounds soon had viewers up in arms. Live baiting, also known as blooding, has been banned in the industry for decades but this footage showed that the cruel means of training Greyhounds was still being used to enhance the performance of the dogs in three states, Queensland, New South Wales and Victoria. Along with the live baiting was the possible corruption and high-level 'cover up' of animal cruelty by governing bodies within the racing industry. Live baiting is seen to give those involved an advantage, enhancing the racing performance of the Greyhound. This does not take into consideration the fact that it carries a high level of cruelty to animals, which inevitably leads to the harm and death of the animal being used as bait. As the industry was being questioned the Greyhound breed was being noticed. Minnie was drawing more and more attention when out and about.

On 22nd December 2015 The Age reported RSPCA Victoria Inspectorate Manager, Allie Jalbert, as saying that 125 criminal charges had been laid for alleged contraventions of the animal cruelty legislation. In Victoria a conviction for live baiting carries a maximum penalty of two years imprisonment or a fine of more than $35,000 for an individual and more than $177,000 for a corporation.

Charges being laid and sentences being handed out also hit the media in New South Wales. Trainer John Cauchi was sentenced to at least a year behind bars before being eligible for parole with his brother Tony receiving an 18 month suspended sentence. Trainer Ian Morgan was sentenced to 12 months' imprisonment after pleading guilty to animal cruelty.

Our home state of Queensland was in the thick of it. Thirteen trainers in Queensland were suspended after the ABC Four Corners footage went to air. According to an ABC News article dated 3rd March 2015 seven of those thirteen were asked "why they should not be warned off race tracks for life and prevented from taking further part in the industry". Five were banned for life, effective immediately, while six others were suspended while investigations continued. A year after the ABC Four Corners program, the number of trainers in Queensland warned off by Racing Queensland had risen to 22. Overall the Queensland Police service and RSPCA Greyhound Inquiry Task Force had handed down 141 charges against 37 people, some of whom were highly respected within the industry.

Trainers Ron Ball and Reg Kay were dumped from the sport's Hall of Fame as they were handed life bans. Tom Noble, a respected trainer from our home town, Ipswich, pleaded guilty to 15 animal cruelty charges. Although presiding Judge Horneman-Wren was quoted in the media as saying, "The destruction of the animal is appalling, it is evident much of the torso is removed. It's not just the attack, or the chasing that constitutes the cruelty, it's the attaching to the lure with the physical and audible distress of the animal and the being hurled around the track." Tom Noble was sentenced to a wholly suspended three year sentence, being banned from greyhound training, unable to own and train dogs and unable to interact with greyhound trainer licence holders (The Queensland Times 6th September 2016). Samantha Roberts, a young trainer of 25, was handed a six month sentence for her participation in live baiting on Tom Noble's property. Julie Edmondson had a life ban cut to 5 years after promising to testify against other trainers with Michael Chapman arguing a life ban would impact his family and social life as he was heavily involved in the industry. What about the impact his actions have had on the animals that were tortured and the Greyhounds who died?

A blow came to those fighting for the rights of Greyhounds and tougher penalties when, in February 2016, almost half of the trainers banned for life in Queensland had their penalties drastically reduced. Joe Braco reported in The Brisbane Times that nine trainers, including those found to have engaged in the outlawed practice had their penalty dropped on appeal to the period of between five to ten years. One has to shake one's head in wonderment as it was reported that Ian Hall, Racing Queensland Chief Executive Officer, refused to rule out the possibility of live baiting still going on. Is there no justice in our system for the animals involved?

Along with the exposure of baiting came the exposure of the finding of mass Greyhound graves. While some dogs were being lured with live bait others were being lured to their death in inhumane and unnecessary circumstances. Not being able to run fast enough or simply not making the racing grade meant cruelty at its worst, being bludgeoned to death, shot, hanged or electrocuted and left to die amongst a mass of other Greyhound bodies. The Sydney Morning Herald (July 20,2016) reported ' that at least 99 greyhounds were brutally killed at a Hunter Valley property and buried in a mass grave over a four-year period because they were 'underperforming' and 'therefore of no further use'." This report came after a Special Commission of Inquiry into New South Wales Greyhound Racing by former High Court judge Michael McHugh. This report found that as many as 68,000 greyhounds had been slaughtered in the past 12 years 'because they were considered too slow to pay their way or were unsuitable for racing'. It was this report that le New South Wales Premier Mike Baird to make the decision to end Greyhound racing as of 1st July 2017.

Many in Australia rejoiced, thanked Premier Mike Baird and began to rally to ban Greyhound racing Australia wide. In statements to the media Mike Baird was reported as saying that "widespread and systemic mistreatment of animals" cannot be tolerated. Besides that of the 68,000 Greyhounds said to be slaughtered over the past 12 years Mike Baird said the inquiry found live baiting to be widespread with about 10 – 20 percent of trainers engaged in the practice. It was found that Greyhound Racing NSW had a policy of deliberately misreporting the number of dog deaths or injuries and the industry was not capable of reforming over the short or medium term. The inquiry found that there were over 6,809 registered greyhounds in NSW which will need to be given consideration with the closure of the industry. The question on everyone's lips was what was going to happen to these dogs. Is it even possible to find homes for this many Greyhounds? How many will be unnecessarily slaughtered? Others were not questioning the future of the Greyhounds but instead the future of the families who, for most of their lives, had relied on Greyhound racing as their source of income. For many trainers it was the only life they knew, having grown up within the industry.

Whilst all of this was happening corporations were listening and taking action with Qantas announcing an end to the exportation of Greyhounds to Asia after revelations that hundreds of Greyhounds deemed 'too slow' were exported to the region. The exportation is in breach of the racing rules and saw some animals suffering in shocking conditions. Animals Australia welcomed the move, labelling the decision a 'game changer'. Qantas issued a statement to the media saying, "We share your concerns about the disturbing story that appeared on the 7.30 Report earlier in the week. The piece was seen by many members of our team. In the past we have transported a small number of racing greyhounds to Asia. However in light of the story we have made the decision to no longer provide racing greyhound freight services to Asia." Qantas is one of two commercial airlines within Australia who freight Greyhounds to Asia, the other being Cathay Pacific who later confirmed they too would no longer be transporting Greys.

The banning of Greyhound racing in New South Wales in no way stopped community outcry as rallies were held to put a stop to Greyhound racing Australia wide. Social media went mad with posts calling for the cruelty to a placid, loving breed to cease. Petitions floated around gaining thousands of signatures. The Chief Minister of ACT soon announced that 'Greyhound racing has no future' and ACT would hopefully soon follow New South Wales. The other states sat watching.

As time passed Australia continued to be divided. Talkback radio was filled with debate for weeks on end. Media from state to state discussed, debated and questioned the ethics of both the industry and Baird. At the time there was talk of the Greyhound industry taking the closure to the high court. This was never required as within three months of announcing the ban Premier Mike Baird backflipped on his decision, announcing the industry would not be shut down but tight regulations would be put into place.

For us the controversy caused escalated attention and discussion when out with Minnie. It was hard to walk past anyone, especially the elderly, without being stopped and questioned about whether Minnie was a rescued Grey. All congratulated us on the use of a Grey, never showing any negativity toward us or Minnie. The discussions varied from those who politely said it was nice to see a Grey used as a service dog to those who wanted to stand for hours and discuss the terrible industry. Then there were those who supported the industry, saying that it was terrible that the live baiting involved the use of the rabbits and pigs but in no way was this the fault of Greyhounds. The fault was that of humans. There is good and bad in every industry but why should an industry as a whole suffer, and Greys suffer, due to a few bad individuals. Of course there was the odd Greyhound trainer who approached us and naturally reassured us that they were not one of the bad ones. They loved their dogs as if they were their own babies.

One thing I found that was never mentioned was the putting down of the innocent Greys, the mistreatment of a beautiful dog, just because it did not run fast enough, could not achieve goals set for it or make enough money for its owner. All spoke of the live baiting but it was rare that anyone spoke of the mistreatment of a dog just because it did not meet standards expected of it by humans in an industry created by greed. Again this involves only a percentage of the industry but is the treatment of this beautiful animal, an act of cruelty by the human race, justifiable in any way? Is it right to harm another species, for personal monetary benefit? These questions could be asked by the racing industry of all animals or any industry that creates harm to benefit humans. It is hoped that with all the outcry and discussion the thought processes of humans are being challenged and changed. It is time society changed its perception of the Greyhound as a dog designed only for racing and embraced them as they do other breeds, loving dogs who offers much joy and companionship.

I watched the news coverage in despair. How could any human allow money to dominate them to the extent that they see the life of a Greyhound to be worthless, to the acceptance that cruelty is an option? How did these trainers sleep at night? I found myself looking Minnie in the eyes wanting to apologise to her for the cruelty other Greys has suffered at the hands of such vicious humans. I found myself cuddling her, letting her know that she will never feel the fear these Greyhounds must have felt.

Within a month of ABC Four Corners exposing the scandal, Greyhound adoption organisations were in turmoil. The initial announcement of the closure of Greyhound racing in New South Wales and the rallying for other states to follow created further rehoming pressure. With Greyhound adoption agencies having a no kill policy this was now a viable and quick option for trainers who wished to retire their dogs. Trainers were now under scrutiny by society, some finding those who would not normally question them asking what they did when retiring a racer.

Greyhounds New Beginnings soon found themselves in a situation where they could not get enough foster carers to meet the demand of dogs being handed over. They could also not adopt out the dogs already in foster care as quickly as the incoming quota. The pressure was on. There was no way this not for profit organisation was going to let the worst of fates come to these Greys. No Greyhound was overlooked as they worked hard finding places for every dog.

# THE PAST LEADS TO THE FUTURE

*An old welsh proverb:*

*"You may know a gentleman by his horse, his hawk and his Greyhound".*

As our journey with Minnie commenced we were to find that there was more involved than just that of training an assistance dog and dealing with the rights to have a dog in a community setting. Having never had a Greyhound before I found a need to quickly learn as much as I could about the breed as questions constantly came to me from members of the general community. A Greyhound in a shopping centre surely drew attention, everyone wanting to know more. Did she have a lot of energy? Don't they eat a lot? Do they have to be muzzled so don't they bite? Is she a great guard dog? I have always thought of getting a Greyhound, what are they like as a pet? And of course the smart comment, has she won lots of races? There was also the question of why they are called Greyhounds when they obviously are not all grey?

The early history of the Greyhound is a hard one to track, with there being a lot of conflicting information online. One thing that is certain is that Greyhounds have a long history which dates as far back as Ancient Egyptian times. While images of the breed are believed to have been sighted in Turkey and on the tombs of Egyptian Pharaohs it is also now considered that it is more likely that the Greyhound originated in Celtic Europe. The ancient Greeks and Romans kept Greyhounds for hunting and as pets, depicting them in their art and mythology, with references to 'Vertraha' (a Celtic Arrian word for greyhound) appearing as early as 8 A.D. We can debate early history as much as we like but one thing we can be sure of is that the Greyhound is one of the oldest purebred breeds around today.

In early history the Greek historian Arrian encapsulated the appreciation for the nature of Greyhounds in his written tribute to 'Horme', his own greyhound. This was as early as 430 BC.

> *"... while I am at home he remains within, by my side, accompanies me on going abroad, follows me to the gymnasium and while I am taking exercise, sits down by my side. On my return he runs before me, often looking back to see whether I had turned anywhere off the road; and as soon as he catches sight of me, showing symptoms of joy, and again trotting on before me.*

> *If I am going out on any government business, he remains with my friend, and does exactly the same towards him. He is the constant companion of whichever may be sick; and if he has not seen either of us for only a short time, he jumps up repeatedly by way of salutations, and barks with joy, as a greeting to us.*

> *Now really I do not think that I should be ashamed to write even the name of this dog... a greyhound called Horme, of the greatest speed and intelligence, and altogether supremely excellent."*

The loyalty and companionship shown in this writing is true of what we see in our Minnie. Wherever Celeste and I are, Minnie can be found, with joy and love evident on her face. When a child is heard crying in distress in a shopping centre, Minnie is searching, ever so ready to offer consolation to whoever may need it.

Loyalty and love towards the Greyhound breed can also be seen in the royal circle, dating as far back as the tenth century where a Welsh King named Hywel Dda (Howel the Good) made a law declaring the punishment for killing a Greyhound the same as for killing a person, which at the time was execution. One could question that, if this law was such in Australia today, the cruelty within the racing industry would not exist.

The first laws that limited ownership to Greyhounds to aristocracy was enacted by King Canute who ruled England from 1016 to 1035. This law lasted nearly 400 years, sadly including the cruel practice of crippling other breeds of dogs so they could not compete with the King's Greyhounds. King Canute's Forest Laws read as:

> *"No meane person may keep any Greihounds, but freemen may keep Greihounds, so that their knees may be cut before the verderons of the forest, and without cutting of their knees also, if he does not abide 10 miles from the bounds of the forest. But if they doe come any nearer to the forest, they shall pay 12 pence for every mile; but the Greihound be found within the forest, the master or owner of the dog shall forfeit the dog and ten shillings to the king."*

> *An approximate modern translation of this is recorded as being: "Peasants may not own Greyhounds only the nobility. Court officers will be sent out to the villages to ensure the laws are adhered to and will sever the tendons of peasants' dogs if they live less than 10 miles from the forest. Anyone found hunting with their dog inside the forest will be fined and their dog confiscated."*

King William I (William the Conqueror, c.1025 – 1087) upheld the ban on commoners keeping Greyhounds, going as far as ordering all non-Greyhounds to have three toes amputated to reduce their speed. King Henry II continued the practice, with the law continuing to be active right up until 1334.

In symbolism the Greyhound can be seen on The Tudor coat of arms as a supporter. It is called the White Greyhound of Richmond and is depicted in many sculptures throughout England. The Corps of Queen's Messengers, who are couriers employed by the British Foreign and Commonwealth Office, carry as their symbol a silver Greyhound. On formal occasions the Queen's Messengers wear this badge on a ribbon and on less formal occasions wear ties with a discreet Greyhound pattern.

King Henry VIII (1491 – 1547) adopted the Greyhound as his personal standard. He owned many Greyhounds, being a lover of hunting and coursing and was the first person to wager on the sport. Today the Greyhound still remains the symbol of the House of York.

When looking at symbolism we also only need look up at the stars where Greyhounds have their place in the constellation, just south of the Big Dipper called Canes Venatici. Conceived by Johannes Fevelius in 1687, the dogs, named Asterion and Chara, are held on a leash by Bootes as he hunts for the bears Ursa Major and Ursa Minor.

Greyhounds have travelled. They were among the 20 dogs that accompanied Christopher Columbus on his second voyage to the Americas, being used not only for hunting food but to subdue the native population. This unfortunately was in brutal ways. As Europeans immigrated to the United States they brought their Greyhounds. In 1770 it was Australia's turn to be blessed with the entry of Greyhounds. Botanist Joseph Banks, on his trip on The

Endeavour with Captain Cook, brought with him a male and female Greyhound. The diary entries of Banks often refer to the regular pursuit of the native animals by his dogs.

Captain Arthur Phillip (who later became the first Governor of NSW) included in his First Fleet, as they sailed into Botany Bay in 1788, his Greyhound and 'assorted puppies'. These were used to hunt the kangaroos that were seen to be damaging the early settlers' crops. These Greys were often crossed with other large dogs such as Scottish Deerhounds and were referred to as 'Kangaroo Dogs'.

By the 19th century the dog population was becoming out of control. This saw the necessity of controlling the population within the new colony. Mongrel dogs were attacking stock, horses and people. In 1801 Governor Philip King ordered that nuisance dogs be destroyed, recommending that people who owned more than one dog should kill them, except for Greyhounds and Terriers. A tax was laid on all "cur" dogs.

Greyhound coursing (the pursuit of game) has been practiced throughout the history of the breed, being used to hunt and eliminate predators. As times progressed, and interest rose, it became a form of entertainment, consisting of two or more sighthounds who pursued a live hare. The first public coursing club was organised in England by Lord Orford in 1776, with popularity growing throughout England and America in the 1800's.

The forming of a coursing club and the popularity within the 1800's was by no way the beginning of the recognition of coursing as a sport. Queen Elizabeth I (1533-1603) was a great lover of the sport, becoming concerned about the unfair advantage the dogs had over the game. In 1561 she ordered 'The Laws of the Leash' be drawn up which included that the prey be given a head start before the dogs were released.

Greyhound coursing was first recorded in Australia in the 1860's initially using native animals until hares were introduced from England. The first club coursing event in Australia was held in South Australia in 1867. The increasing popularity of Greyhound racing in the 1920's saw a decline in the popularity of coursing. The use of live prey was eventually made illegal in Australia, with the last event being held in South Australia in 1985.

With horse racing being known as the sport of Kings in the early years, Greyhound racing soon became the sport of the Queens. Greyhound racing as it is today can be seen as having its origins within coursing with 'The Laws of the Leash' by Queen Elizabeth I being the precursor to the industry. The first attempt at racing Greyhounds on a straight track happened in England in 1876, being unsuccessful with the coursing enthusiasts. The modern racing of today that uses a circular or oval track can be seen as first starting in America in 1912 with the invention of the mechanical hare by Owen Patrick Smith. The English soon noted the popularity and profitability, building a track on which they held their first race in 1926.

1927 saw Greyhound racing commence in Australia. The Lang Labor government amended the Gaming and Betting Act to allow legal wager, the Greyhound Coursing Association was formed and the first race, using a 'tin hare', also known as the mechanical lure, took place at Epping Racecourse (renamed as Harold Park in 1929 to prevent confusion with the Sydney suburb of Epping). While horse racing continued to lure the wealthy, Greyhound racing soon attracted the working class man due to the low admission charges, ability to place small bets and the holding of races being at night or times that suited their leisure hours.

An American fad saw a different take on Greyhound racing in the 1930's where Capuchin monkeys were trained to ride the dogs. This often included hurdles and water jumps. Specially designed saddles with harness were used with the monkeys wearing miniature jockey silks. A photograph shows this event being held at Shepherds Bush, Mascot, Sydney, back in 1930, with it continuing to be in practice in Australia up until 1950.

So what of the name Greyhound? It is generally believed that the word stems from that of the Old English grighund, hound being the modern version of 'hund'. The meaning of 'grig' is still today undetermined. With the Greyhound being seen in a wide variety of coat colours one can only assume that there is no relationship between the Grey within Greyhound and the colour grey, nor is there any indication that the origin of 'grig' and the colour grey are associated. According to Julius Pokorny, an Austrian-Czech linguist (1887 – 1970), the English name Greyhound does not mean 'grey hound' but simply 'fair dog'.

Many versions of the Bible, including the King James version, name the Greyhound as one of the 'four things stately' in the Proverbs. However some newer biblical translations have changed this to a strutting rooster. To us Minnie is surely stately but with her long muscled legs and sleek body we would definitely not relate her to a strutting rooster.

# A BREED MISUNDERSTOOD

With a lot still to be discovered about the origin and past of the Greyhound, confusion and misunderstanding continue to loom in society. With many states still requiring the owners of a Greyhound to have their dog muzzled when in public, it is a misconception that this breed is vicious and one to be cautious of. This is far from the case. The muzzling of Greyhounds was introduced into Australia in 1927, initially being introduced on the race track to prevent the dog from injuring itself during the general excitement at the track or during their high speed sprint. There are no muzzling laws in USA or UK. Muzzling is a controversial topic with groups rallying to have the law lifted. In 2013 the Dog Act in Australia was amended to allow for Greyhounds to undertake 'Green Collar' testing. This test assesses the dog's temperament, testing that it shows no aggressive or dangerous behaviour around small animals. Should the Greyhound pass this testing it is issued with a numbered 'Green Collar' which when worn in public exempts it from being muzzled. Greyhound muzzling is a breed specific law legislation which does not take into consideration the individual dog. On their website the RSPCA state they support the complete removal of requirements, saying it has *major ramifications for greyhound rehoming, preventing many Greyhounds that are discarded by the racing industry from finding a new home. Removing muzzling laws*

*would significantly help improve the image of Greyhounds and thus help increase rehoming rates'.* Some council areas within different states of Australia have lifted the need for a muzzle on any Grey whilst it is in their council jurisdiction.

We knew nothing of the breed when Minnie first came into our life. I had never owned a Greyhound nor was I into Greyhound racing. When I think about it I had gone through my life not even giving the Greyhound any thought until I came across Todd McKenney's Greys. Celeste had definitely never seen or patted a Greyhound. Her first introduction to Greys was when she watched videos of Todd's Greys on Facebook. The possibility of us getting a Grey lead to further internet searching, discussing the racing industry, the retirement of Greys and the adoption process. Celeste was already very much aware of saving the life of an animal through adoption as animal shelters were where most of our pets had come from. It was always the first point of call when we had room to offer a new animal a home. It was even a point of call when seeking a Grey.

We were lucky enough to be surrounded by the support of the Greyhound industry, being made welcomed into the family long before we even had Minnie. It was this support, and the willingness of Todd McKenney and the Greyhound community to answer my never ending questions that I was able to put my doubts aside and find the love that is on offer from a Grey. The Greyhound community joke is that once you get one Grey you will surely get another as the breed is truly infectious. This would soon be shown to be true in our case as later we were to foster Minnie's sister Rena.

Greyhounds make the most adorable and loving pets. They love nothing more than to curl up on the lounge or your bed for cuddles. If it is soft and comfy you can be guaranteed your Grey will be the first one to find it. In our house there is a daily battle for the lounge with Minnie looking at us quite indignantly when we tell her she must move. When the lounge is not on offer and it is free time for Minnie you will often find her on the bed. Dog beds are available but how dare we insult Minnie and suggest she use them. Anything soft is Greyhound domain.

Greyhounds are large dogs that vary in height, ranging from 68cm to 76cm, with males naturally being taller. Minnie is on the small size for a Greyhound, hence her name originally being spelt 'Mini'. We decided to change the spelling of her name when we first got her as we felt being labelled small all your life not befitting. With the spelling of the name changed we soon found a Minnie Mouse collar which Celeste agreed was very suitable for our girl.

Along with their sleek bodyline is a muscular rump and long skinny legs. Still today I look at Minnie's rump in awe. How I would love to have such a muscular frame. A comment I often get is that of how soft and smooth Minnie feels, this being one of her calming sensory attributes. The coat of a Greyhound is short and shiny. Like other dogs they do shed hair but very minimally, making them ideal for those with allergies to dog hair. They need minimal brushing and do not get the doggie smell of most dogs as their coat is not as oily. With less oil in their coats, Greyhounds do not need to be washed as regularly as other dogs. Washing too often strips the coat of its natural oils, drying out the coat and skin.

Greyhounds have a reputation for having a very high energy level but this is far from the truth. Yes, they run, but only for a few minutes a day, being designed as sprinters not as marathon runners. They require one or two short bursts of activity (known as zoomies) a day, sleeping 16 to 20 hours. Minnie engages in zoomies in the morning when she first goes outside and then again at around 4pm. Our backyard is small, approximately courtyard size, yet Minnie still tires herself easily, running up and down the thin strip of grass. A couple of times a week we take her to the off-lead dog park where she runs madly with the other dogs.

With a lot written about never allowing your Greyhound to run off-lead due to them having a strong prey drive, and the fact that they can see for almost a kilometre, it took me a long time to gain the confidence to allow Minnie to run with other dogs. Although she is trained for recall, the information given to me by owners of the breed had me convinced she would not come back when in a large open area. Todd McKenney has also put many videos on his Facebook page of his dogs at the park off-lead, mentioning that they love to run but it is no use calling them as they will not return until they are tired and ready. The dog park we take our dogs to is not fenced but is equivalent to an island, being surrounded by water with bridges to enter and exit. My concern was that she would follow other dogs, ignoring my commands to return. Over a period of time I tested her until I had gained the confidence to give it a try. I should never have worried. She never strays far from us, enjoying the free run with Celeste. When she tires she heels alongside Celeste and me off lead, showing no interest in roaming. Greyhounds love to meet and greet other dogs and Minnie is no exception. She loves her afternoons at the dog park, crying as we approach the park in anticipation of the run. The smile on her face and whimpers of delight as she sniffs the other dogs' butts warms our hearts. Naturally Minnie also gets a lots of exercise walking around when out with us and on the days we are out and about her zoomie is not required as she is exhausted from the missed hours of sleep. One of the disadvantages of only having a small area for your Grey to do zoomies is that they dig up the grass as they quickly turn to run back the other way. As Minnie runs you can see bits of grass flying out from under her. This is still the case when she runs in large areas but the damage to the area is less obvious. If you have ever seen a Greyhound running you will know of the speed they achieve in such a short time. It is this that causes them to become exhausted very quickly.

With this fast run, naturally comes thirst and heating of the body. Like all dogs Greyhounds need to have a supply of water on hand at all times and also love to cool down by placing their feet or body in water. Minnie loves to sit in the lake at the dog park after she has had her run in order to cool herself down. When at home a wading pool is a great place to have a swim. The other extreme for a Greyhound is the cold. With sleekness comes lack of body fat and relatively thin skin. The general rule with Minnie is that if we need a jumper so does she.

Part of adopting an ex-racing Greyhound is definitely that of understanding the industry they come from and what is involved in the day in the life of a racing Grey. Racing Greys are born into the industry, having been bred from a purebred racing line. Both Minnie's mum and dad were racing dogs. I have been lucky enough to have continued contact with the family who bred Minnie from close to the time we got her. They are a lovely family who over the time of us owning Minnie have been open with information on Minnie's history. For myself it has been lovely to be able to have them travel this journey with us. It is through them that I have been able to understand Minnie better, getting the information needed about her early years.

Minnie was born in Rockhampton on 13/1/13 in a litter of 8. Her start in life was that of a being small one, weighing in at only 292 grams, the smallest of the litter. She fitted into an ice cream container. It was not a relationship of love for Minnie's parents but one of convenience, the insemination taking place artificially using frozen sperm in a straw, from sire, Bo Frazier, which was implanted into bitch, Spring Malawi, in a vets surgery.

Minnie was registered as a racing dog with Greyhound Racing Victoria but unlike two of her brothers and two of her sisters she was never given a racing name, instead being registered as unnamed. She was never to see the track. She was broken in at the age of approximately 13 months but just wasn't fast enough. By 17 months she was ready to be adopted.

Ex-racing dogs have never been pets, being housed in kennels. They have never known the life of a close family or the comfort of a human house. All of this is new to them when they are retired. It is unrealistic to expect a Greyhound who has only ever known kennel life to understand the rules and functionality of a human house. Many have never seen stairs. Minnie did not like stairs at all. Going up wasn't too bad but there was no way she was going down. When it came to stairs, not only did the decline and height look scary but those long legs just got in the way and became wobbly when going down. Celeste was determined to show Minnie that stairs were okay, crawling up and down them while she spoke softly to Minnie, encouraging her to follow. Minnie would sit at the top of the stairs enjoying the companionship and entertainment but you could see the 'you have to be kidding' going through her mind. With the help of Smart Pups Minnie now handles stairs like a pro.

Greyhounds can be very sensitive souls, initially having to get used to the sounds and loud noise of a house. When I was first told that Greys could be like this I worried that they would not be suitable as assistance dogs as in this role they needed to be calm and under control. At first Minnie would jump at any noise and 'rear up' on-lead as a horse would. The fright and flight instinct would set in if the noise was extreme. I didn't need to worry about this for too long as with the training from Smart Pups she takes her job seriously and has a strong level of trust in us so now takes noise in her stride. Celeste is very noisy, especially during a meltdown. With this verbal loudness comes that of banging and lashing out. Minnie proved to us from day one that this was not going to be a problem. Instead of running from the noise she would stand at a distance and observe. These observations of hers quickly led her to understand what was happening, better than I think I will ever understand, and she would rush to the aid of Celeste, offering calmness. The fright and flight reflex has never been seen in relation to Celeste or any other human. The initial issue was only noises made by outside influences, such as a metal speed humps banging as a car drove over it in a car park.

One small problem we did have with Minnie when she first came into our life was that of stopping and freezing when it came to walking into confined spaces. This made it very difficult each time I wanted to get her into the car when in a carpark as she refused to walk between our car and the car next to us. I spoke to her racing owner about her training for the 'box', feeling that this must have been hard for her, but was reassured that she trained with ease. I never really did work out why confined spaces were a problem. Perhaps it had something to do with being crated from Rockhampton to Brisbane, approximately 619 km's, to be put up for adoption. Thankfully it did not take Smart Pups long to reassure Minnie that entering a confined narrow space was not an issue and today she is fine.

Another thing we had to teach Minnie, and in my opinion at the time was that it had to happen really quickly, was that when you lived in a house as a pet you did not need to wake up and go outside as soon as the sun thought about rising. I have since found that this is not an isolated case just applying to Minnie. When in training a Grey's morning starts very early. Minnie would come up to the side of the bed, nudge me and lick my face at around 5.30am telling me it was morning time. She would not leave me alone until I got out of bed and let her out into the backyard. At first I thought she needed the toilet, with house training also not being something racing Greys have learned but something you must teach them. However toileting was never her issue. She just wanted to smell the fresh morning air, go for a walk and have a quick zoomie around the yard. In the beginning I would wait for her to do her business, calling her and willing her to come inside as the mornings were chilly. Who was I kidding? She is a Grey. The laid back nature of the Grey meant she had no care in the world about what I wanted nor any care about coming when called. I quickly learnt that regardless of the cold it was best to leave the back door open and go back to bed, leaving Minnie to do her morning thing. She eventually came inside, tongue hanging out, tired from her zoomie but as happy as Larry. I would find my sleep disturbed and myself wide awake, but Minnie had achieved what she needed and once again curled up on the soft bed to fall asleep. Thankfully she never woke Celeste, but why would she when I was an easy, gullible target. Slowly as the days passed, and I wised up to her ways, I made her wait longer and longer each morning, until we came to an agreement that 7am was more than early enough. 8 am on the weekends was fine.

Toilet training Minnie so that she could be an inside dog was not a real issue. I have had many dogs who take weeks, if not months, to get the idea. For Minnie it was a matter of a few days and she had it all worked out, either holding on until someone opened the door or standing at the door asking to go out. This was the beginning of her showing us she was a quick learner.

The greatest concern from all of the Greyhound adoption organisations I approached was that of our cats. Cats are small and fluffy just as is the lure Greyhounds chase when racing. It is a natural instinct of a Grey to chase a moving object, with some Greys becoming so fixated that nothing will distract them. When you adopt a Greyhound from Greyhound New Beginnings you are given a muzzle. We were advised to keep the muzzle on Minnie at all times when she was around the cats as she had not been cat tested, meaning it was not known how she would react. Minnie was naturally curious about our cats, approaching them with muzzle on and sniffing them but in no time at all they were best friends. Each time Minnie approached the cats with muzzle on I would speak softly to her telling her to leave it and praising her for doing so. At first we placed her on-lead allowing her to sniff and discover whilst we had control. The lead was soon removed and then, once I was confident, the muzzle. Initially the muzzle was only removed when Minnie was under full supervision. With trust came the ability to watch them at a distance and then leave them in a room alone with confidence.

We only ever had one incident between Minnie and the fluffiest of our cats, Milly, but thankfully no one was harmed. Minnie was quietly sleeping next to me in my office when Milly walked past the door. On this occasion Minnie forgot her manners, jumping up to chase Milly. There was a terrible hullabaloo as the cat took off with dog in pursuit and myself following behind yelling at Minnie to leave it. Being inside it did not last long as the cat found a bed to retreat under. Minnie, knowing she had done wrong, spent some time sulking because I had raised my voice to her. Greyhounds are gentle by nature, having a tendency to sulk. For the rest of the day Minnie would look away from the cat when it was in her vision, showing me she was sorry and could be good.

The day before she had done a similar thing. She was at the rat cage sniffing around unmuzzled. She was told to leave them and directed away from the cage. For the rest of the afternoon she would only look at the cage from a distance. Minnie had only been with us a matter of days when both these situation happened. For myself I was certain she had the ability to be a Smart Pup, all under control.

Then there is the relationship between Minnie and our other cat Jimbo. Jimbo came into our lives less than a month before Minnie, at a time when the Animal Welfare League, overrun by cats, were having a reduction in the price of cats for the weekend. That weekend we were going to look only. We already had a cat so did not need another. Every parent knows how it goes. Once the kids see the cute kitties and the kitties see the kids you are doomed. Jimbo chose to be Alex's pet and there was no way Alex was going to let us leave without him. He followed Alex around the cat room, hiding under things at Alex's feet and ever so gently touching him with his paw to let him know he was there. When Alex looked at him he gave those beautiful little 'I love you' eyes that no parent can resist. Yep, I am a softie and the kids and cat knew it. Apparently cats choose their owners too. Today the relationship between Alex and Jimbo is as priceless as that between Celeste and Minnie. Cats offer just as much therapy as dogs but on a totally different level. Whenever Alex leaves his room Jimbo can be heard meowing and is seen pacing looking for him. He nuzzles Alex just as Minnie does Celeste and sleeps by his head every night. He rarely leaves Alex's room or the house.

The relationship between Minnie and Jimbo was one that took us by surprise as Jimbo is a skittish cat who prefers either the company of Alex or his own. No other human besides Alex is able to get close to Jimbo as he runs and hides yet the bond between Minnie and Jimbo was one of instant love. At the time of introducing Minnie to the cats she showed a lot of interest in wanting to go into Alex's room. At first I thought she had a need to get to know Alex but I soon realised that Jimbo was the attraction. She would stick her head in the door every time it was open, slowly edging her way closer and closer to where Jimbo was lying. Jimbo never made any attempt to run from Minnie, instead sitting quietly looking at her as though to welcome her. It was only if I entered the room with Minnie that Jimbo would scamper. I soon began to take this a little personally but was assured it was just the way Jimbo was.

In no time at all the love between Jimbo and Minnie became sickening. Everywhere Minnie was Jimbo was. They would rub noses and heads and curl up on the lounge together with Jimbo sitting between Minnie's front legs right under her nose. My heart would be in the pit of my stomach every time they were together as I waited for Jimbo to come off the worse. Here was this greyhound which I was led to believe had the potential to eat cats, and a cat that could be seen as pleading to be eaten, curled up together. There were many times I caught Minnie grooming Jimbo and Jimbo returning the favour. At times I wondered if Jimbo was a little confused and thought he was a dog. The love between the two is a love that continues. I am not sure if Jimbo thinks he is a dog or Minnie thinks she is a cat but it is pure love and adoration.

I soon came to the conclusion that it was not cats that Minnie would chase but the sight of something fluffy. Jimbo was a short haired cat whereas Millie was a long-haired, fluffy cat. It was not so much that Millie was a cat but more that her tail stood high in the air waving its long fluff around for the taking. Today Millie and Minnie get on well with Minnie no longer taking any interest in the fluff.

Minnie showed the whole family immense love from day one. Her calm and quiet nature, the fact that she rarely barks or makes a sound, is soothing to the body, mind and soul. Minnie has really shown that with a little bit of patience and a lot of love Greyhounds make the most amazing pets.

# A FRIENDSHIP THAT WAS MEANT TO BE

Minnie has always been our perfect little package. Being small makes her an ideal match for a little girl. I don't think we can go out without receiving the comment, 'She is very small for a Greyhound' or, 'Is she a whippet?'. I once asked Minnie if she ever felt embarrassed about being referred to as a whippet. I came to the conclusion, by the smile on her face and the way she holds herself, that she feels six foot tall and proud. She has every reason to be proud.

To watch the relationship blossom between Minnie and Celeste has been nothing but magical. Celeste was very aware that we were collecting Minnie as her dog, with the hope of her being suitable for training. She was also aware that Minnie was only under foster care and if she did not suit would need to be returned. I often wonder if all this had any effect on the instant bonding between the two. The two of them were determined from day one to show me that Minnie had to stay.

Over time, as I look back, I realise how much Minnie assisted Celeste from the very beginning. At the time I was sure I was seeing instant changes in Celeste, with confidence in herself being the biggest one, but wondered if I was imagining it. It was more than just the cuddles in the car driving home and Celeste tucking her in with pillow and blanket the first night. Minnie had brought with her some sort of magic that filled Celeste's day with love and joy and mine with hope.

Looking back at my Facebook status updates the first week after we got Minnie, I can only reflect and smile. Each day I would place an update, letting everyone know how she was going.

Day one 16th March:

> *'Minnie is settling in well. She has snuggled onto what she seems to have claimed as her lounge chair and Mummy Celeste has tucked her in again.'*

A little later that same day I posted a photo of Celeste and both our dogs with the status:

> *'Celeste reading (telling) the animals a story. One dog on the lounge, one on the dog bed behind her and the rats covered snugly in their cage. She is such a good mummy.'*

Here was Celeste, a child who at the age of eight was not reading and showed little interest in books as they caused anxiety and meltdowns, spontaneously telling a story to the dogs. I watched with excitement. She proceeded to open the book and, while showing both dogs the pictures, told them her version of the story. I didn't say a word as I did not want to disturb her and break the moment but also because I was speechless. When she finished reading I very quietly commented that it was a lovely story and shared the moment with her, discussing how relaxed the dogs looked and how she was a lovely mummy. Her face lit up and I saw a degree of confidence I had never seen before. She sat tall and proud with a huge smile on her face. I could not believe my little girl had taken it upon herself to look at a book and to actually share it with someone, even if it be animals.

The Facebook status updates over the next few days continued with:

> *'If it is soft you lie on it and wait as eventually Mummy Celeste will cover you over.'*

> *'If you get uncomfortable wiggle yourself into a more comfy position then look pleadingly at Mummy Celeste until she tucks you back in.'*

> *'I walk into the room and this is what I find. Two munchkins watching cartoons.'*

> *'Tonight Celeste chose her favourite knitted blanket to cover Minnie with. This tucking Minnie in on the lounge has already become an after dinner ritual.'*

For a child who is self-centred and unable to see the needs of another, Celeste was showing care for Minnie from the moment they met. Minnie offered no judgement, just acceptance of what Celeste was doing, enjoying every moment of her company. Any fear of failure or confusion that Celeste may feel when associating with another human was not evident when she interacted with Minnie. From day one I praised Celeste for her gentle care of Minnie, reinforcing the appropriate caring behaviour. We would discuss how we thought it made Minnie feel and how it makes us humans feel when someone does something nice for us. One of my fears here though was that Minnie was already becoming a bit of an obsession. The routine of covering her over each night was quickly set in concrete, with my fear being that should we have a night of Minnie not cooperating or a blanket not being available a meltdown would be inevitable. A little thing to some but a huge thing for me because, at that time, I lived in fear of the consequences of routines becoming unbalanced.

Then there was this status update:

> *'I am very proud of Minnie again today. She is showing herself to be very affectionate and caring. Celeste was outside stimming (banging her head) in frustration. Minnie was standing nearby and seemed to notice so went up to Celeste and nudged her. Celeste stopped to pay Minnie attention. With a huge smile Celeste told me that she was angry and hitting her head but that Minnie had helped her feel better. I stood there amazed. Minnie seems to know what she is here to do.'*

Words cannot describe how I felt on this occasion. Minnie had not even started her training nor had I given her any command of my own, yet here she was, doing exactly what she was going to be trained to do.

There was another occasion where Celeste was unable to cope, taking herself outside to run the yard while head banging and screaming. Knowing it was not a time for me to get involved, as my involvement would only cause further anxiety, I let her go alone, watching that she was not going to get into any harm. Celeste had only been outside a short period of time when Minnie went out to find her. As soon as Minnie reached the back stairs and noticed that Celeste was struggling she took it upon herself to approach Celeste and gently nuzzled her side with her nose. Celeste stopped running and head banging and leant down to pat Minnie. When she stopped patting, Minnie would nudge again. Eventually Minnie sat down next to Celeste who then fell to the ground in a big embrace with Minnie. When Celeste was ready both walked quietly inside. Celeste went on to another activity quite calmly with Minnie nearby for the rest of the day. I praised Minnie for her good deed without making too much of a fuss in front of Celeste as the last thing I wanted was to reinstate any anxiety or sensory issues. Quietly, inside, I was shouting with joy and jumping up and down. Yes! Minnie had done exactly what I had dreamed of.

# A LITTLE BIT OF ORGANISATION AND A WHOLE LOT OF LOVE

How scary it must be to arrive at the home of a family you do not know and be faced with smells, sounds and an environment you have never experienced before. There is no secure kennel to be locked in at night, your meals have changed and the bed you are used to is gone. You find yourself in a human house when the cement floor of a kennel is all you have ever known. For Minnie this was the reality when she arrived at Greyhounds New Beginnings from her home in Rockhampton. She then found herself making another adjustment as she was sent to a foster carer, to be returned to Sarah at Greyhounds New Beginnings where she was picked up by us. She then arrived to a house full of many animals and to facing the challenge of proving to us that she was the dog for the work we had in mind. With her calm and gentle nature she seemed to take it all in her stride not knowing at the time that the pressure had only just began. There were many more challenges in front of her as she was given the responsibility of being the first Greyhound to be put through the Smart Pup Program. The future of other Greys as Smart Pups assistance dogs was on her shoulders.

Having raised our $20,000, conversations were flowing to and fro between the office of Smart Pups and myself. I decided to inform Smart Pups of my current situation concerning both the money and the dog, asking if they would be interested in training Minnie as an assistance dog. A reply to my email was something along the lines of the office staff liking the idea but they did not know anything about training dogs so would send my enquiry to Patricia McAllister, the director. To my relief I was not fobbed off in the first instance.

The afternoon of the day of my email to Smart Pups I decided to take the kids to the movies. While in the movie I placed my phone on silent, putting it in my handbag. As we were walking back to the car I checked my phone and there, shining brightly on my screen, was the first part of an email from the office of Smart Pups. Only being able to read a few words I was sure what I was reading was only my imagination. As I opened the email fully my excitement escalated. There in black words on the screen of my phone was a great big YES! Smart Pups would be honoured to give Minnie the chance to be trained as a Smart Pup. Woo Hoo! Yes! Yes! Yes! Things were going our way and we were finally on our journey to a certified assistance dog. I drove home as quickly as I could, sticking to the speed limit of course, to text my daughter, Sam, and Todd the exciting news. I also jumped on the phone to let Sarah know that Minnie had found her forever home. Of course there was still the chance that Minnie was not suitable or would get so far into her training and fail. Should this have been the case I had made the decision that Minnie would be ours regardless. It was impossible, and unfair, to break the strong bond between Minnie and Celeste.

As we settled in, conversations and emails with Smart Pups progressed and the plan of training Minnie as the first Greyhound Smart Pup assistance dog were put into place. Minnie had been assigned a trainer, Claire, and we were to meet her and Patricia at Chermside Shopping Centre. They would bring a training jacket for Minnie and we would put her to the test. The idea was to see how she reacted to people, sounds, smells and crowd. With Smart Pups being located on the Sunshine Coast and myself being located in Ipswich this was an ideal midway point for both. This would be the test that would give us a definite yes or no as to Minnie's suitability. Without Smart Pups seeing Minnie and knowing what her temperament was they could not commit to training Minnie but instead had only said they would give it consideration. This was also an opportunity for them to meet Celeste and observe the relationship between her and Minnie.

I clearly remember the day being a Wednesday. It is not due to Wednesday having any significance but more that I remember it was mid week and I remember how nervous I was. We were moving into the next stage of acceptance into the Smart Pups program. I was so grateful to Smart Pups for even considering Minnie as this was not the norm for them. A part of me was saying that I knew this was going to work but there is always that nagging doubt.

It was a 50 minute drive to Chermside Shopping Centre but it felt like hours. It was mid afternoon so the traffic wasn't too bad but every car in front of me annoyed me. Minnie took the drive in her stride, sitting on the seat beside Celeste, resting her head on Celeste's car seat, keeping her little girl calm. Alex, Celeste and I arrived before Claire and Patricia and had to wait a while. We were in a Brisbane council zone where the law said Minnie must be muzzled. I felt sorry for her as she looked at me with pleading eyes asking me to remove the metal contraption that was unnecessarily on her face. Everyone who passed us stopped for a chat. Most commented on the muzzle mentioning they were aware of the law and that it was ridiculous. Discussion led to other breeds of dogs who were vicious yet not required to be muzzled. A few questioned why she was muzzled and were surprised that the council saw it necessary. Little did I know at the time that this was the beginning of being approached by strangers for a chat on a regular basis.

While waiting for Patricia and Claire it became very hot. The heat began to heighten Celeste's anxiety, which was already rather high due to being out and about. Celeste began to head bang and again Minnie stepped in, approaching her and nudging her. Celeste was soon sitting down on the ground with Minnie next to her having a cuddle.

Patricia and Claire arrived with two Labrador Retrievers who were at the end of their training. We popped an 'in training' coat on Minnie, with her showing relief that I was able to rid her of the muzzle on her face, and proceeded into the shopping centre were we sat to have a drink and brief chat. We chatted about the program and their thoughts on adjusting it to meet the needs of Minnie and our family. Whilst I spoke to Patricia, Claire took Minnie for a walk around the centre. Upon returning she commented on how well Minnie had performed, taking everything in her stride, but that she had she frozen near stairs. I told her of my similar experiences at home. As far as Smart Pups were concerned this was not an issue at this stage as it was something that they could work on. Short term and long term goals were discussed. We then proceeded as a group to walk the three dogs around the centre. This allowed Patricia and Claire to see the relationship between Minnie and Celeste. Again Minnie excelled. This dog could not put a foot wrong. The whole time we walked around the shop she leaned towards Celeste and stayed close to her side. Celeste naturally walked next to Minnie stroking the top of her head to keep herself calm. Patricia commented on the amazing relationship the two had established in such a short period of time. There was no pressure placed on Minnie to perform at this stage, the aim was to see her natural ability. She coped with people and noise as though she experienced shopping centres every day. We stopped at the top of stairs and escalators with Claire and Patricia taking their dogs up and down, the aim being that Minnie would watch them and see how it was done. As I watched Minnie's reaction I was sure she was thinking they were very clever but we had to be kidding if we ever thought she was going to risk her life and go down those damn things.

Our afternoon ended on a high with Claire and Patricia agreeing that Minnie showed heaps of potential. They did reinforce that even the best dogs fail at the last minute but they were happy to give it a try. The next stage was a one month trial after which, if Minnie learnt the basics, it would be full steam ahead. It was arranged that as soon as Smart Pups received the cheque from The Courier Mail Children's Fund I would attend the Sunshine Coast for three nights where Minnie would be taken through some basic training, I would be taken through the basic commands and we would receive our 'in training' jacket. I would then train Minnie and meet with Claire regularly who would give Minnie new skills that I would maintain until we saw her next. This was not how Smart Pups usually do it but they were writing a new program just for Minnie. With the bond between Celeste and Minnie already being strong and the benefits Celeste was already receiving evident they did not feel it was a good idea to take Minnie into their care and break the bond. Should I not be able to handle the training or if it seemed not to be working then plan B, that of placing Minnie in the care of Smart Pups, would be put into place.

That evening I received a lovely email from Claire.

> *Patricia and I really enjoyed meeting you and your*
> *lovely children today. We look forward to getting to*

*know you all better and working with you in order to benefit Celeste's development.*

*We found Minnie to be a lovely, well balanced dog and as we discussed can see a lot of potential in her successfully qualifying as an assistance dog for Celeste.*

*I understand there were many ideas suggested and some training information discussed at our meeting today so I would like to clarify what was decided and agreed to, to prevent any confusion.*

*Smart Pups has agreed to commence training Minnie on a one month trial basis. Over that month we will be able to establish whether Minnie can cope with public access training and also whether the long distance, training relationship will work for all involved.*

*To commence the training I will need time to work with Minnie in a low distraction environment to establish her obedience training and you will need lessons in handling Minnie in public while she is in training. To achieve this we have offered for you to come to the Sunshine Coast for three days in April.*

*Until we begin Minnie's training you can work on marking off her socialisation records and practicing leadership skills at home. I have attached a sociali- sation record for you to check off and fill in. I have also attached some leadership information for you to read and begin to put into practice. The information relates to a puppy in training and Minnie is now becoming more mature however all rules still apply. You will receive more information during the initial three days of training.*

*To begin with we discussed giving affection as a reward. Minnie needs something to motivate her to work, so in order to encourage her to work for praise and affection you need to only give her pets when she offers behaviour you want to encourage. This does not mean that you can never pet her when you have the urge, it just means that if you want to pet her you can ask her to sit or come. Further down the track she will be able to follow many more commands that you can reward her for.*

*We also discussed her diet and agreed that no changes needed to be made.*

*If you could please confirm the training dates, we can arrange your accommodation and send you an itinerary for the 3 days.*

*If you have any questions please email me and I will get back to you as soon as I can.*

Of course I could confirm the dates. I was going to move mountains to make this work. If Smart Pups wanted me there on a particular day then all other affairs would just have to wait. The date of the 21st April was set down as day one. This worked well as Alex had a birthday on the 25th meaning that Sam would be in Queensland. She would travel with us to the Sunshine Coast looking after Celeste so I could concentrate on learning my part of the training.

The wait for the cheque seemed to be a long one that kept the April date for commencement of formal training in limbo. There were other things on our mind while we were waiting.

Two weeks prior to the start of Minnie's training Celeste had an operation to remove a majority of her teeth. For reasons unknown to the orthodontic team, Celeste's baby teeth had decayed from the gum down. The specialist stated it was not the normal decay due to not brushing but could not explain what was causing the issue. Although Celeste was not giving us any indication of being in pain we had no doubt that she was. Her mouth was a mass of black holes, some very close to the root. Being her baby teeth the best and healthiest form of attack was that of removing all the decayed teeth. This would only be day surgery but for a child with sensory issues and high anxiety it was not an easy task. With Minnie not yet being a certified assistance dog she would have to stay home. This was dealt with by reassuring Celeste that Minnie would be there to curl up with her as soon as we arrived home. To replace the comfort she would miss in Minnie we took a trip to the shops the day before where Celeste chose a special teddy to keep her company.

The drive to the hospital the morning of the operation only took 15 mins but it seemed like a lifetime. Celeste was a mess. She had worked herself up so badly that she threw up in the back of the car all the way to the hospital. Throwing up due to anxiety is not uncommon for Celeste so a supply of vomit bags are always kept in the car.

Once we arrived the nerves calmed a little as I occupied her with the toys in the waiting room. She was visited by the specialist and nurses who all spent time talking to her and making light of the situation.

The walk down the corridor to the operating theatre felt like walking the hallway of death. I do not know who was more nervous, me or Celeste. Any parent will know that to see your child go through any operation, no matter how minor, is not an easy thing but to see the fear and confusion in your child's eyes makes it worse. Upon arriving at the theatre table, all hell let loose. The little bit of calm Celeste was holding onto disappeared as she screamed and threw herself around the room. The anaesthetist insisted she lie still on the operating table so he could put a cannula in her arm and administer the medicine. I looked at this man with disbelief. I can't remember what I said to him but I am sure it was something along the lines of "Are you kidding me?" I do remember telling him to just do it as I cradled Celeste tightly in my arms and a nurse held her arm. As soon as the anaesthetic was administered she was sleeping soundly. I gently placed her on the theatre table and left the room, walking back to the waiting room as instructed to await the specialist's assessment. I do not remember feeling upset but instead feeling a sense of relief that Celeste was at peace in her drugged sleep. As I sat in the waiting room chair a sense of exhaustion hit me. I felt as though I had run a marathon.

The specialist and a nurse soon came to see me and gave me the rundown on the procedure. He had taken a good look in Celeste's mouth while she was under, observing that he would need to remove most of her teeth. He again stated he was baffled by the form of decay and we would need to keep a close eye on her teeth to watch that it does not happen to her second teeth. He said they would be a few hours and suggested that I go and get a coffee. I remember him asking me not to be too long and requested I sit just outside the recovery door as they may need to call on me as she awakes. I noted the grin on his face as he said this.

I knew the moment she woke and so did the whole of Ipswich. She went down fighting and came up fighting just as furiously. The nurse opened the recovery door and called me in. What I saw as I walked into the room was something I will never forget. Here was my little girl with tubes coming out of her and an oxygen mask on screaming and throwing her body around. Standing around her were about half a dozen nurses trying to hold her down. She was screaming, "Let go of me," and "Don't touch me". As I entered a masked man standing at the end of the bed, who I soon learnt was an anaesthetist, looked at me and said "Good here's Mum, maybe she can do something with her." As I looked at him he said, " She is all yours." When I think back at this I wish I had been thinking more clearly as my response would have been that she was their responsibility at this current moment in time, not mine.

As I approached the bed I asked the nurses, maybe a little too forcefully, to take their hands off Celeste. One of the nurses abruptly said that they needed to hold her down to prevent her from hurting herself. I thanked her kindly and said I understood her concern but they were escalating the confusion and causing Celeste to rage further. By holding her down they were causing panic and by touching her they were causing sensory overload. As they released Celeste she calmed slightly and they all looked at me with amazement. I spoke softly to Celeste, stroking her hair, which I knew she liked but not touching any other part of her body. My poor baby was a mess. Blood was pouring from her mouth. She had terror written all over her face as she came in and out of consciousness. Her face was like a balloon and red with tears. Keeping a calm voice I hummed to her, noticing that a degree of calmness had crept into the room. Most of the staff left, leaving only two nurses.

The rages continued for the next 30 minutes with the nurses eventually getting permission from a doctor for an injection of an anti-anxiety drug. Eventually, as Celeste regained consciousness and the drug set in, we were able to place her on my lap while I sat on a chair and the nurses could attend to the blood that was constantly filling her mouth. I used a wet flannel to gently wipe her mouth and face. Taking the oxygen mask off her face relieved one sensory issue. She would rage occasionally in my arms saying her mouth was dry and she needed a drink but when offered water, ice or a water ice block she would rage again, saying that she could not let anything touch her mouth.

Things settled to the degree that Celeste was moved to the ward where she would be observed for a few hours. If she ate something she would be allowed to go home. Ate something! The poor child had just had half the teeth in her mouth taken out and had a mouth full of stitches yet they wanted her to eat something. Were they serious?

So the battle began. They placed dinner in front of her which consisted of a piece of steamed fish, mashed potatoes and veggies. Dessert was a tub of ice cream. Celeste refused to eat, crying and saying she wanted to go home. She was sore, tired and they were pushing her to the limit. The tantrums continued as the nurse kept coming back into the room every 5minutes to check if she had eaten and make comments saying she could not go home unless she ate. I was about to explode. I kept asking the nurse nicely if she would like to eat if she had a mouth full of stitches. I again sat Celeste on my lap on the chair, cuddled her in my arms and told her all was okay. I suggested she try to eat some of the ice cream which had now turned into milk. With the use of a straw we sipped the ice cream and declared to the nurse that we classed that as eating. A new nurse had come on by this time as the sun had set and night was upon us. The nurse looked at me and smiled, declaring that yes, we could go home. Victory to us!

We gathered our things and slowly made our way to the car. At first I wondered how I was going to get to the car as Celeste was heavy and we had a distance to walk. She bravely, yet slowly, walked for me, just feeling pleased to be going home.

The night was not yet over. We arrived at the automated machine to pay for the parking and when I put my ticket in it kept spitting it out telling me my ticket wasn't validated. What! I took the ticket out of their damn boom gate. I was tired and furious. I had a child who was tired and in pain standing next to me. Due to the hour, the carpark was not manned and without a verified ticket I could not open the boom gate to get my car out. I don't know how many times I put the ticket into the machine to have it spit it out at me before an elderly couple walked up to validate their ticket. I told them the problem I was having but their ticket went through okay. The lovely couple, who I am sure could see the frustration and despair on my face, helped me find a number to ring. Connecting with a human on the other end, who informed me was security, I was told to drive my car to the boom gate and he would manually open it for me. At least I got a free park.

While all of this was happening, Alex was at home animal sitting. He had rung me previously and asked me what to feed the dogs so at least that had been taken care of. Knowing it would be a tough day I had prepared the day's meals for Alex the day before so at least I knew he had also eaten. When we arrived home I swear Minnie had a smile on her face from ear to ear. She completely ignored me and went straight to her girl. Celeste fell into bed with her arms wrapped around Minnie. Minnie lay with Celeste all night without moving.

The morning revealed a sore and grumpy girl. There was also constant vomiting as the blood had run down Celeste's throat overnight and the anaesthetic was still in her system. For a good few hours Celeste threw up and slept and then threw up some more. I rang the hospital and was informed this often happened but if she was still sick by lunchtime to bring her back. No one had mentioned this possibility when we left the hospital.

All morning Minnie lay on the bed with her girl, a look of concern on her face each time Celeste sat upright to vomit. Each time she lay back down, Minnie would push her body against Celeste offering comfort and Celeste would wrap her arms around her.

As the vomiting wore off Celeste progressed to a bed on the lounge where she could watch TV. Minnie did not need to be told to follow and curl up with her. There was no way anyone was going to split up this dedicated team.

The next few days were spent relaxing and coming down from the anxiety caused by the operation. Although we had left the hospital, the anxiety was not over. There was anxiety from the pain and anxiety that if she moved her mouth stitches might fall out. Every few minutes I was asked to check her mouth to make sure it was okay. What was that dried dribble on the side of her mouth? What if the liquid she drank caused the stitches to fall out? Prior to going to hospital I had stocked up on custards, yoghurts and all things soft and liquidy. These were all that were consumed for a few days until I could eventually take her mind off her mouth and onto other things. I look back now and realise how much I called upon Minnie for pats and cuddles during those few days. Without Minnie I would not have been able to do anything. With Minnie I was able to leave the room for a few minutes to go to the toilet, make a cup of coffee and attend to daily tasks. The love shared in the household was not only between Minnie and Celeste. As the days passed I began loving this dog more and more. She was my saviour, my angel from above who was taking a life full of hell and giving us a little bit of heaven.

The day Celeste woke and decided she could now play was a day of relief. This was not only for me but I saw it in Minnie's eyes as well. You could see the excitement on her face. She was pleased to have her friend back again as they played the morning games. Minnie showed that she understood what was happening. She understood that Celeste was sick and needed her and that her role at the time was to patiently sit and be with Celeste. She may not have been happy about it as she really wanted to do zoomies around the back yard and run with Celeste but she knew that it was about Celeste healing, not about herself. I noticed that during the time Celeste was lying around, Minnie did not ask to go outside to toilet and when I took her out she was hesitant. I needed to reassure her that I would watch Celeste while she went to the toilet. If we take the time to listen to animals, to watch their body language and to feel their emotion we can truly see that they understand more than we give them credit for and show a deep compassion for their owners. For Minnie it was clear that she knew her role was to care for Celeste and that already she saw me as the master, the one who told her what to do and fed her. As the week progressed and the training began this would be more evident as she tested me and pushed me to my handler limit.

# LET THE TRAINING BEGIN

As the 21st April drew closer and the date of the commencement of training loomed we seemed no nearer to seeing the cheque. I started ringing The Courier Mail Children's Fund and so did Smart Pups. A few days before the training date, to the relief of all, the cheque came through and plans to commence were confirmed.

While waiting for the official training I had taught Minnie to sit using treats. This resulted more from Minnie being a natural than from my trying hard. Each time I wanted to pat her or we were outside we would practice. Beauty already had to sit and wait while I put her food bowl down. She knew to wait until I said okay, after which she would run to her bowl to eat. The same rule applied to Minnie, with Beauty role modelling. Her eagerness to get her food caused a lot of failure and also confusion as she approached her food and I took her back to where she was and got her to sit. It took teamwork to accomplish this one. I would stand next to her holding her by the collar while maintaining command, praising her. Celeste would put the food bowl down after which I would follow with the okay command, letting go of her collar. It took a while but we soon succeeded. We also worked on stairs. Celeste continued to walk and crawl up and down the stairs, with Minnie up the top, encouraging her to join her. Eventually she got to the stage where she was trying to take a step to follow Celeste, wagging her tail and smiling. We managed to achieve getting her to step her front legs down two stairs by placing a treat on the second stair, but her back legs just would not follow. The rest was up to Smart Pups.

Celeste continued to flourish each day as she focussed on Minnie, not the tasks at hand. Puzzles of any kind were always a frustrating challenge for Celeste. I remember the day I gave her a floor puzzle which consisted of large cardboard pieces. As she sat on the floor Minnie lay down next to her. With a giggle Celeste divided the pieces of the floor puzzle between Minnie and herself – one for her, one for Minnie...She started by placing a piece of her puzzle in front of them both then looked at Minnie's pile of puzzle pieces to see if she had a piece that would fit. During the process Celeste would continually ask me to look at the good job Minnie was doing. I would praise Minnie while mentioning that they were working well as a team and without her help Minnie would not be achieving. The to and fro of my turn your turn continued, with Celeste talking to Minnie and problem solving, until the puzzle was complete. No tantrums and no help from Mum, just a huge grin from ear to ear and a cuddle for Minnie. I proceeded to take a photo of Minnie and Celeste next to their completed puzzle. Magical Minnie had done it again!

The day before we commenced training we found ourselves at the airport picking up big sister Sam. Due to the intensity of the three training days and the fact that I really needed to concentrate, Sam had flown from South Australia to come to the Sunshine Coast with us. Being a single mum with no family close, the cost of the airfare was our only option. It was always nice to have Sam visit. Celeste loved to see her sister and relished in doing the things sisters do.

The drive to the airport went as could be expected. With Minnie not officially in training we were not able to take her so Alex decided he would stay home and keep her company. Celeste threw herself around in the car due to the trip being 45 mins. Requests by Celeste to turn the radio down led to abuse to turn the radio up, which led to abuse to turn it down again. The back of my seat was kicked numerous times whilst she screamed, saying she was going to vomit, the normal reaction to anxiety. The 45 minute drive felt like weeks. By the time we got to the airport Celeste was a mess and my stress level was at boiling point. As soon as I had parked the car I headed for The Coffee Club. The biggest and strongest coffee they could make was needed.

When we collected Sam from the airport we did not enter the building as the noise and hustle and bustle of human traffic would have caused confusion for Celeste. Having to place her favourite toy on the conveyer belt for it to pass through security would have caused anxiety and incessant talking to herself. When I was alone with her I could not ask her to wait on one side of the security scanner and then walk through to me. With security not allowing two people to walk through at the same time, this was an issue. Occasionally when Sam is departing we will go with her to see the big planes as then I have her help at security but upon arrival it is easier for us to meet her outside. On the odd occasion, when the drive to the airport is smoother than can be, I will attempt to take Celeste inside to the main foyer and we will sit by the baggage collection point and watch the conveyer belt go by. This eliminates the need to go through security, lessening the sensory and social stimulation, yet gives Celeste a different experience. This also allows us to sit and watch the flight number on the board waiting for it to tell us Sam has landed. I realise how much I play a balancing act and how much Autism controls our lives when I write of things such as this. We go inside, we go outside and I do all I can to keep Celeste's mind occupied and free from anxiety in the name of peace and quiet for all. Staying outside and waiting can cause anxiety and meltdowns with Celeste incessantly asking when Sam will be here. Going inside can cause the same behaviour due to sensory overload and anxiety as to why the flight number is not showing a green landed sign. When you are dealing with a child with autism you never know which way to go. Sometimes you can do something and all will be fine. Next time you do what you see to be exactly the same thing and all hell lets loose, leaving you scratching your head wondering what went wrong. It is physically and mentally exhausting. When out you must be on the ball at all times. Your focus must be on the child, ready to divert the next overload.

When it comes to the airport, The Coffee Club is always my saviour. While I refuel with my stress-breaking coffee, Celeste is happy to sit with a piece of cake and a milkshake. On this occasion we didn't have long to wait before Sam arrived and we were on our way home. The trip home went a little more smoothly as Sam's presence kept Celeste talking and interested in what her sister had been up to.

This was the first time Sam had met Minnie. Like all those who meet her, Sam was surprised at her small size. I think it was safe to say that she fell in love with Minnie instantly. Minnie has a way of doing that to people. There is just something about her calming nature that puts people at ease and attracts them. Definitely, by the end of our days away, and by the time Sam left to return home, Minnie had a place in her heart.

The trip from home to Buderim on the Sunshine Coast, where the dog training was to take place, was 1 hour 30 mins. It was an early start the next morning for Sam, Celeste and me, as we were to meet Claire at 9am. Alex was staying home to look after the animals. The idea was to get in as many hours training Minnie on the first day as we could.

Fearing the worst with Celeste, and predicting peak hour traffic, I left us plenty of time for breaks. The trip went reasonably well. This time Minnie was by Celeste's side, ready to comfort her when needed. We were to go straight to the dog training park and would book into our motel at the end of the day.

The plan for the three days was that Claire would take Minnie and work with her whilst I went to shopping centres with a Smart Pup who was at the final stage of training and another trainer. I was shown the commands and taken through the steps required to train a Smart Pup. Celeste and Sam tagged along and spent time at the shops while we trained.

I soon fell in love with Chevy, the beautiful golden retriever who was given the job of showing me how it all worked. With a smile that lit up his whole face and a wagging tail that showed plenty of love, Chevy took me under his wing, gently letting me know that he was willing to be patient and abiding while I learnt the ropes. I was surprised to find it all quite easy. Using common sense and a strong command I soon got the hang of how to be boss, or perhaps it was Chevy who made me feel that way. Chevy and I walked our way around the shops like pro's. I said sit and Chevy sat. I said leave it so Chevy left it. When we sat for a drink Chevy kindly went down out of the way of other shoppers and waited patiently. Celeste strolled behind with Sam, giggling to herself in awe of Chevy.

Each day there was time for a break which we took advantage of, visiting Mooloolaba beach. At first we did not dare venture onto the sand fearing that this sensory stimulation, along with the events of the day, may be too much for Celeste. At the best of times, the sand and salt of the sea water caused Celeste to itch, which caused anxiety and agitation.

At the end of day one Minnie was given her Smart Pup training coat, meaning she was now part of the Smart Pup team and our training journey was official. Minnie was now also part of our personal team. She could officially go with us everywhere. This meant that Minnie was legally accepted in our motel room and we could take Minnie with us to dinner by the beach.

After the completion of our first day of training we drove directly to our motel. This was a short drive from the training grounds and was a small motel meaning that the noise and stimulation within the surrounding facilities was kept to a minimum. Our room consisted of two double beds and a set of bunk beds. With the first day concluding mid afternoon, we had time to explore the surrounds of the motel. This included the pool which was to cause me a slight headache over the next few training sessions as Celeste's insistence to swim lead to anxiety. The incessant talk began with wanting to get in but not being able to as she was too anxious. The depth of the pool was an issue. A leaf in the pool floated by and a bug fell in, leading to incessant anxious screams from Celeste as we could not reach the bug and save it. When reassurance was given for one thing another anxiety causing issue was found. Minnie stood on the edge of the pool as I tried my best to keep Celeste calm. Celeste sat on the step of the pool not being able to get out and not being able to get in any further. In situations like this she is opposed to everything I say. If I speak I am adding to the overload in her head. If I don't speak her mind caves in as it whirs away with its own thoughts and anxiety sets in as she yells at me for not speaking.

Eventually, with time, and after a headache on my part, something clicks in Celeste's mind. She makes sense of the environment around her and she calms. It is only then that we can work together as a team and come to an agreement of what we should do. This, naturally, is a discussion led by myself as I guide her to an acceptable outcome. Of course our afternoon didn't just end with the pool meltdown. Having to leave the motel to get dinner, anxiety over what we were having for dinner and of course the age old decision of having to decide what bed to sleep in and coping with the fact that it was not her bed and that the routine was different all fed her anxiety. Thank you ABC Kids TV for keeping your program schedule consistent. No matter where I go ABC Kids TV, or the Ipad app, is my saviour. When your world is changing, just having that one little thing that has not changed can be what makes it a little bit easier.

On the last training day we again finished early and a treat was in store. We took Celeste and Minnie down on the sand for a run through the waves and a dig in the sand. Minnie took the feel of sand under her feet in her stride. I need not of worried about how she would react. She stepped onto the soft sand as if she had done it a hundred times before. As we approached the waves she stood by Celeste, helping her manage the noise, different texture and uncertainty of the water. We did not live near the beach so this was all new to Celeste, who coped extremely well as she held onto Minnie. Little was I to realise at the time that this experience was to lead to heaps more beach fun in the future.

The last day of training also saw me leave the Sunshine Coast with a spirit full of even more confidence. What Claire had achieved teaching Minnie in only a few short days was amazing and reinforced the intelligence of a greyhound. I may have taken an ex-racing greyhound with me to Buderim, a dog that was not used to the obedience tasks she was put through, but I surely was not leaving with the same dog. When we first got Minnie I was surprised at the way she walked on a lead, heeling nicely beside you, often leaning on or brushing against your leg. I have heard other Greyhound owners also speaking of the natural ease of walking a Grey. Although Minnie had showed a natural ability to do this it was evident that Claire had taken it one step further, creating a dog who not only stayed close but was alert and ready for the next command at all times. Within a short period of time Minnie showed a clear understanding of the command ' this way', turning with you in the direction of command. The following of more complex commands such as 'sit' and 'down' were slow but this was also something that I had to work on, getting the giving of the command to a level that I was confident with. There was still a lot of training to go but I had no doubt that Minnie could do it. Claire continued to reinforce that Minnie could fail at any given moment as the tasks asked of her became harder. My heart told me Minnie was made for the job.

After an exhausting few days we set off on the long drive back to Ipswich. Minnie was exhausted but there was no letting up for Celeste.

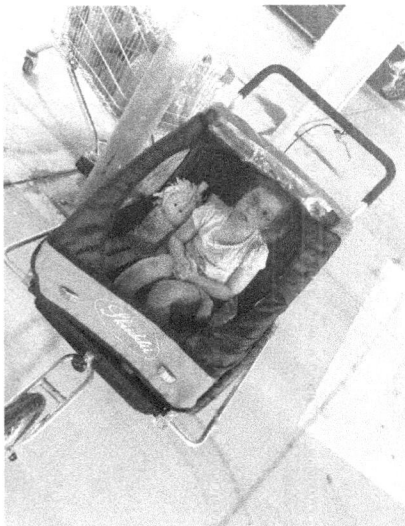

The bike buggy kept Celeste secure and happy when out but was cumbersome.

A special meet and greet with Celeste's hero, Batman. Movieworld, Gold Coast.

Taking Minnie home for the first time. The connection between Celeste and Minnie was instant.

The bond between Minnie and Jimbo was one of instant love.

Meeting Todd McKenney for the first time prior to seeing Anything Goes at the Queensland Performing Arts Centre (QPAC).

Celeste sits in the backyard calmly contemplating life with her two best friends, Beauty and Minnie.

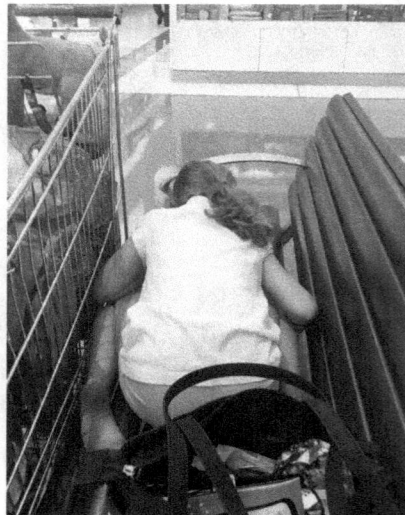

Shopping prior to Minnie took time and patience, hiding and meltdowns being a regular occurrence.

Judy Sharp (author, A Double Shot of Happiness), Tim Sharp ( Laser Beak Man ), Jennifer, Celeste and Minnie.

A happy family moment prior to heading out to see Anything Goes.

Prior to Minnie coming into our lives a trip to the shops was full of sensory overload. The calmness and acknowledgment of the world around her seen in these photo's shows the huge difference Minnie makes.

A calming cuddle with big teddy when we visited 'Sonata in Z' by Dawn-Joy Leong, Nick Waterlow Gallery, UNSW Art and Design, Paddington, Sydney. This bear travelled the trip back home with Celeste.

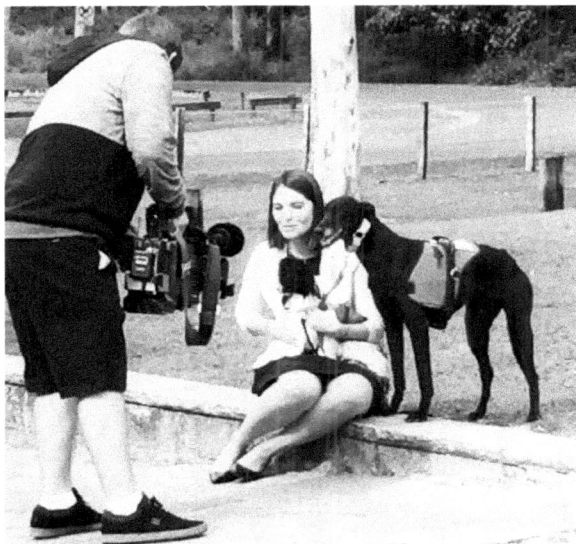

Minnie has her moment filming with Win News, Sunshine Coast, Queensland.

Ready to be there for Celeste if needed during swimming lessons.

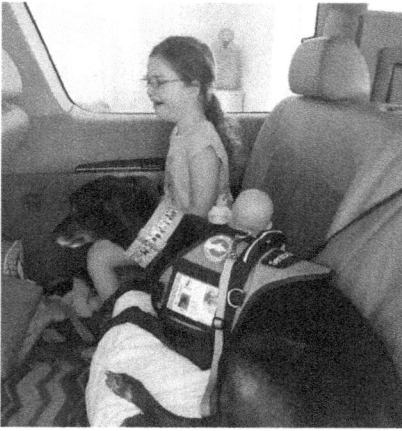

The not so good and the good moments travelling in the car.

With the help of Minnie photo's with Santa get better every year.

Celeste and Rufus. Animals play a large part in Celeste's life.

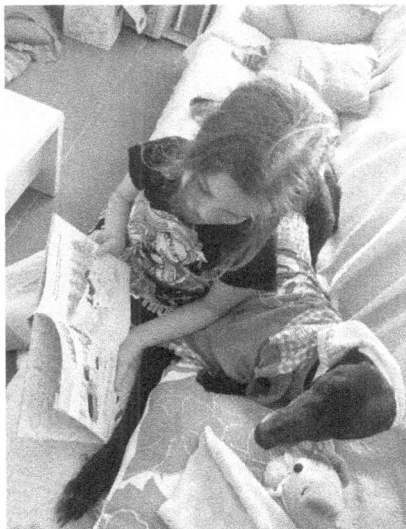

Celeste reads her baby a bedtime story.

Taking Celeste on a trip to Sydney would have been impossible without Minnie by her side.

Supporting Greyhounds New Beginnings at a fundraiser.

Bedtime is much calmer with Minnie.

The Dynamic Duo.

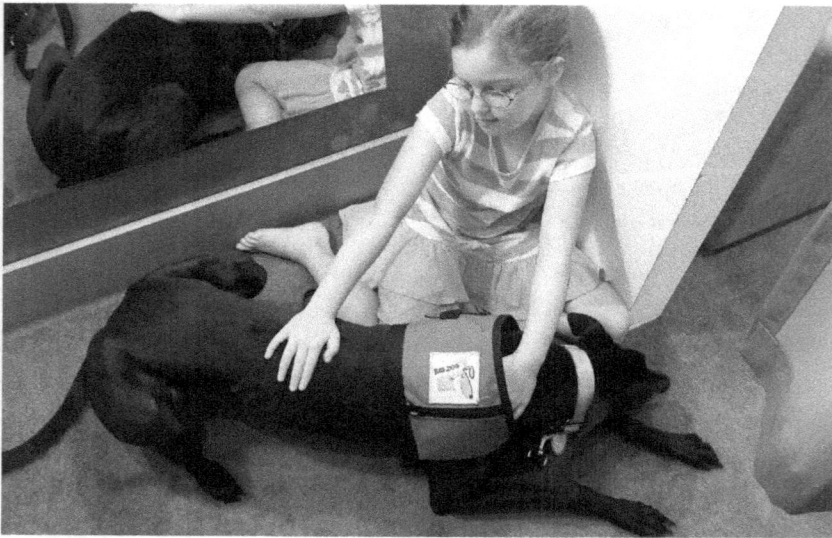

The early days of training. Minnie shows she has what it takes to be an assistance dog. Minnie keeps Celeste calm whilst I try on clothes in a department store.

# UNDER MY COMMAND

A week would pass before we were to meet with Claire again. This may not seem long but it was a daunting time for me with the pressure on, not only for myself to remember the training but for me to make sure that all went well with Minnie and that she continued to follow direction. We now never left the house without Minnie. The days we did not go out Minnie was put through her training in the back yard. There were also the stares, judgement and questions from the community to deal with along with the questioning from shop owners who were either not aware of the law or who doubted Minnie was in training. No one had seen a Greyhound assistance dog before so Minnie drew a lot of attention.

I won't lie and say that this first week was easy. It took a bit of adjusting to having Minnie with us all the time. I now had two responsibilities and extra things to consider. When building places or planning events, humans do not give consideration to the presence of dogs. When taking an assistance dog there is a lot to consider but I was soon to find that the benefits of Minnie soon outweighed the considerations.

I once had a lady approach me in Woolworths and tell me how lucky I was to be able to bring my dog shopping with me and that there are a lot of people who would like to try the same thing. This lady was being sarcastic and rude, having a dig at the fact that we did not look as though we required an assistance dog and Minnie surely did not look like an assistance dog. This is a common occurrence as people look for the obvious disability signifying the need for the dog. With all the kindness I could find in my heart, I spoke to her gently, explaining Minnie's role, making sure I made it clear that the responsibility of an assistance dog is not something to be taken lightly and that to have a dog in a shopping centre is also not something that is necessarily easy. I hope that this lady took home with her a little bit of knowledge and education on assistance dogs and will in future think before she sprouts such comments.

Still today people approach me to ask me what the role of Minnie is. We are fine with this as it is only by asking questions that the community will become educated. I actually prefer a few moments of my time to be taken up with polite conversation than to be stared at or to listen to the exchange of misinformation between two parties. It is important to remember though that Celeste, Minnie and myself are a three-way team, meaning that I do not have the disability but have the capability of handling questioning. This is not the case in the situation of a dog who is assisting an adult. In most cases the dog is led and commanded by the person with the disability. Consideration needs to be given to the disability.

The first week of being out and about with Minnie by ourselves went smoothly. Minnie took it all in her stride. The thing I found the hardest was not due to anything Minnie did but due to my own adjustment. It is not until you are in situations like this that you realise how much you do things by routine. We quickly get comfortable doing things one way and are thrown out of kilter when changes are needed. It made me realise how difficult it must be for someone with Autism who needs such strict ritual in order to prevent confusion. Minnie was not yet able to do stairs, escalators or travelators, meaning that I needed to consider where I parked the car when attending shopping centres, making sure that if it was underground or multi-storey parking there was a lift or ramp. Even though Minnie now does stairs and travelators this is still something I need to consider as it is not an easy task getting a heavy trolley full of groceries, a dog and an anxious child on and off a travelator. We were coming into winter so returning to a locked car was not a high consideration at this time but would become one when the warmer months hit. The heat of the bitumen was also to be considered as when returning to a hot car I could not leave Minnie standing waiting for the car to cool down before I put her in. The pads on the feet of dogs can easily blister. The safety and wellbeing of Celeste was always first priority when out but I had now added the safety and well being of Minnie. I soon realised that having Minnie was like having another child, except that this child did not fit the norm of social behaviour, raising eyebrows and questions.

At the end of the first week we once again met Claire at Chermside Shopping Centre. This time Claire was accompanied by Andrea, another trainer who would be involved in the training of Minnie. With them was one of their dogs who, like Chevy, helped me go through the paces. This time I was to learn to manoeuvre escalators, stairs and lifts. Minnie stood with Claire and watched us. With the previous experiences of Minnie and stairs we were not getting our hopes up that she would follow lead with Claire. It surely was hard keeping my excitement under wraps when she followed the other dog, walking down three flights of stairs. The stair phobia had finally been broken. Here I was thinking it was going to take months, if we ever managed it all, and within a couple of weeks she had it. I was also excited to hear

Claire say that Minnie had maintained all she had learnt at the initial training and that I was doing well with my commands. Maybe now I could relax a little, although there was still a lot to learn.

So with stairs being accomplished there was still one other thing that concerned me, that of toileting Minnie. Although I had never had any issues with Minnie urinating or defecating inside the house it concerned me that she would be out with us all day and would need to learn to hold her toileting. It was a case of encouraging her to go to the toilet when we went outside. This is something I had been doing at home. I would put her on the lead and take her for a walk before bedtime giving her the command of 'quick quick' which is used by Smart Pups for toileting. Although it was early days Minnie had yet to toilet while on lead but as soon as I took her off lead she would go. Part of the passing of certification as an assistance dog was toileting on demand and while on-leash. Like all things I need not have worried as it soon proved to be something I was doing wrong and not her, as Smart Pups had her doing the deed on the command of 'quick, quick.' before I had time to sneeze. I was beginning to wonder if there was anything the Smart Pups trainers couldn't teach a dog to do.

If you ever see someone standing with their dog on a lead saying 'quick quick' please do not consider that they may be mad. It may look and sound strange but I can assure you there is a reason for this. Beauty has been trained to toilet on command for as long as I remember. It was something that I had taught her as a pup so I could not understand why I struggled with Minnie. I would allow her to witness Beauty toileting on command hoping she would get the idea but no luck. It took me a while to get used to the command 'quick quick' as for Beauty I used the more likely words of 'wee wee', at which she would also poo, so to her it just meant 'toilet'. Now today I must say 'quick quick' and then 'wee wee' in order to give two dogs different commands. It was soon mentioned to me that Minnie is a lady. Claire noticed that although she will toilet on command she is hesitant and prefers to do it where no one is watching. She rarely poos on command instead, holding on and when the opportunity arises taking herself to a private area where no one can see her. Even dogs have dignity and seek privacy.

The day of our second visit to Chermside Shopping Centre was a long day as Celeste had swimming lessons that afternoon. Celeste had been attending swimming lessons for over a year. Not only was the plan to achieve that of learning to swim but also that of socialisation with her peers. The latter was not to be achieved. From day one Celeste cried at swimming, although water was her therapy. When it was a hard day at home we would fill the bath and she would play in the water for hours. Some days she would get in and out numerous times. Celeste could be melting down one minute but once she was submerged in water the worries of the world were forgotten. The problem with group swimming lessons was not the water but a combination of being touched by the other kids, having to understand the social cues of the other kids and her auditory processing deficit causing difficulties and confusion with following directions when in a group.

After 6 months of being placed in and out of group lessons it was decided that the therapy of the water and the safety of learning to swim were more important than the socialisation. One on one private lessons it was to be. Socialisation was achieved to a degree with Celeste making friends with Thomas, a boy who was a year younger than her and also had Autism. Each week Thomas would have a lesson in the lane beside Celeste. We all agreed that this was a non-threatening way to introduce socialisation. Before long Thomas and Celeste had become friends, spending a few minutes running around together before their lessons. During lessons they could be seen competing with each other to see who could swim the best and furthest. It would be interesting to see if the relationship between Celeste and Thomas changed with the introduction of Minnie as Thomas's mother had stated he was not keen on dogs. This is something I would soon learn was common in children as parents walked a wide birth around us in shopping centres. We have had kids freeze, cry and constantly look over their shoulders in fear to see if we were following them.

This particular afternoon was the first afternoon Minnie would be introduced to our lessons. Swimming was held in a large shed type building that consisted of two pools. Our half an hour lesson was held at 2:30pm, a time when the swimming centre was at its quietest as the other kids were only just getting out of school. By 3:00pm the noise had started and we were pleased to be getting dressed and leaving. Again Minnie took it all in her stride. I sat at the side of the pool with Minnie in a down position and she sat and watched Celeste. In the situation of Celeste having a meltdown and jumping out of the pool I would approach her with Minnie and give the nuzzle command. Over a period of time there was no need for me to give Minnie the command. She was always on watch, jumping up should Celeste get loud or seem upset. The noise of the other children at 3:00pm never worried Minnie, who soon became the superstar of the pool. With Minnie on the side of the pool the meltdowns soon stopped. If her teacher saw one coming a quick reminder to Celeste that Minnie was watching, and a glance by Celeste across to Minnie, was all that was needed to calm her down.

Not only was Minnie the superstar of the pool but she also became a star at the local shopping centre. I was soon to learn that Ipswich had a huge Greyhound racing industry, with a lot of trainers in the area. It was at the Ipswich court house that charges against trainers were being laid. To attend the shopping centre was to be stopped by many to discuss the industry and to tell me their stories of their families' racing Greys. All were quick to tell me that their family was one of the good ones and would never harm an animal. I was quick to state that I was not willing to discuss the racing industry as my role with Greys was to train Minnie as an assistance dog and hopefully have other Greys following her. I was surprised at the number of people who would approach me and ask me if Minnie had won lots of races and made me lots of money. I was quick to point out that the jacket she had on was an assistance dog jacket and not a racing jacket. This led to a quick, and embarrassing, get away by the person.

Then there were those who were interested in the pilot program and would thank me profusely for adopting a Greyhound and giving her a second chance. These were the discussions I enjoyed, the ones with people who were willing to be educated about not only the breed as a pet but also their intelligence. These people also took a moment to learn more about assistance dogs and Autism. I could only hope they were telling their family and friends about Minnie, the program, Greys and the great work an assistance dog does.

# ASSISTANCE DOGS AND THE LAW IN AUSTRALIA

Australia wide, it is recognised that people with disabilities often require the support of an assistance (service) dog. Even with this recognition and laws in place granting assistance dogs access to all places humans visit, with the exception of certain parts of health service facilities and parts of a public place where food is ordinarily prepared, assistance dogs can be met with hostility, judgement and discrimination. I understand that not all humans like dogs, with some even being fearful, but what needs to be remembered here is that these dogs are not pets, they are working dogs who are trained at particular skills and who have a high level of discipline. They deserve the respect they have earned during training and through the day to day assistance and companionship they offer their handler. The assistance dog industry is highly regulated with fines and penalties for those who are seen to do wrong. A legally certified assistance dog must wear its jacket with certification badges when working. When certified, the owner is presented with identification cards which must be carried with them at all times and presented upon request. The person with the disability (primary handler) holds a card and in the case of the primary handler being a minor an alternative handler card is issued to the adult who supports the primary handler. This is known as a three part team. The team must be together at all times while the dog is working in a public place. I cannot take Minnie to the shops without Celeste as her job is to assist Celeste.

In Australia, accreditation of assistance dogs varies from state to state with differing governing bodies. The one thing all assistance dogs Australia wide have in common is that they come under the banner of The Disability Discrimination Act 1992 (Cth) (DDA) Section 9 which sets out the legal definition of an assistance animal as a dog or other animal that:

(a) is accredited under a State or Territory law to assist a person with a disability to alleviate the effects of disability; or

(b) is accredited by an animal training organisation prescribed in the regulations; or

(c) is trained to assist a person with a disability to alleviate the effect of the disability and meets standards of hygiene and behaviour that are appropriate for an animal in a public place.

In our home state of Queensland, Minnie is certified under the Guide, Hearing and Assistance Dog Act 2009, with amendments being made in 2015 (Guide, Hearing and Assistance Dogs Amendment Act 2015).

Within the Act the objects are stated as being:

(a) to assist people with a disability who rely on guide, hearing or assistance dogs to have independent access to the community; and

(b) to ensure the quality and accountability of guide, hearing and assistance dog training services.

These objects are stated as mainly being achieved by:

(a) protecting the right of people with a disability who rely on guide, hearing or assistance dogs to be accompanied by the person's guide, hearing or assistance

Within the Act a disability is describes as person's condition that

(a) is attributable to—

    (i) an intellectual, psychiatric, cognitive, neurological, sensory or physical impairment; or

    (ii) the presence in the person's body of organisms causing illness or disease; and

(b) results in

    (i) a reduction of the person's capacity for communication, social interaction, learning, mobility or self care or management; and

    (ii) the person needing support.

(2) The disability may be, but need not be, of a chronic episodic nature.

Under the law it is illegal for any individual or business to deny access to an assistance dog. Individuals in control of a public place or public transport vehicle, such as a waiter, bartender or taxi driver can be fined up to $11,000. Privately owned businesses such as restaurants, hotels, shops, taxis, theatres and sports facilities can be fined up to $55,000. It is the responsibility of an individual and business owner to be aware of these laws.

Most people relate an assistance dog to that of the labrador or retriever commonly used as a guide dog. This is no longer the case. An assistance dog can be of any breed but is easily identified by the coat it wears that is adorned with the relevant certification badges for the state it resides in. Coats worn by dogs vary in colour and design depending on the organisation they have been trained with.

Minnie wears a coat of red which is clearly labelled 'service dog', carrying the Smart Pup badge along with the Guide Dogs certification badge. It is clear she is a service dog and by whom she has been trained. If an individual or business is unsure of the authenticity of the coat they are able to politely ask the handler for the identification cards, which in our case are displayed in a clear plastic pocket on the side of Minnie's coat.

# A LITTLE BIT OF EDUCATION IS OFTEN NEEDED

Life is all about learning. Open communication and education are the keys to success in all we do in life. This is something I have always believed and something I have found to be true when out and about with Minnie. Overall we have been very lucky in the attitude of others towards us. On most occasions our experiences are pleasurable and having Minnie has meant we have had the opportunity to enrich our social interaction...but like all things there are always rotten apples in a barrel.

Our first rotten apple came some months into Minnie's training. It came in the form of a confrontation with security and centre management at our local shopping centre. It took me by surprise as, being the largest shopping centre in the Ipswich region, boasting over 100 specialty stores along with a medical centre, I would have thought their professionalism and knowledge of the assistance dog law to be that of a high standard.

What really surprised me in this situation is that for months prior to this hiccup we had been attending the shopping centre with Minnie in tow without a question from management. Security had been passing us, glancing at her coat, smiling and saying hello. The local community had embraced Minnie with the owners of the retail shops being welcoming. Being regulars at the centre we had made friends with the other regulars and I was soon known as the lady with the Greyhound.

The incident started as I was sitting in the food court with Minnie and Celeste. We had only been at the centre a short period of time when Celeste had a meltdown. Time out is always a good idea so I decided to take Celeste to a quiet corner of the food court with a drink so we could chill out for a moment. Just as my bum hit the seat a security guard came toward me at a quickening pace. By the look on his face I could see he was looking for trouble. Not being one who seeks trouble, and always being aware that when out and about Minnie is representing Smart Pups, I smiled warmly at the security guard, saying hello. Before he could even say anything I reassured him that Minnie was a Smart Pup in training, bringing her coat to his attention. He nodded, said he just had to check and left. Confrontation diverted...or so I thought.

Within a matter of a few minutes he was heading toward me again with huge strides and determination. As he approached he spoke into his two way radio. I stayed seated and this time remained quiet, not offering the previous friendly conversation. Standing above me he asked me if he could see my identification cards. I again politely gave him a rundown of the situation and what Minnie was being trained for while handing him our identification card. After once again speaking into his two way radio he stated he would need to take my identification to centre management. He left, leaving me sitting there scratching my head. By this stage Celeste was becoming anxious about the situation, being unable to cope with the sensory overload of what seemed like a reprimand.

It was some time before the security guy returned with my identification. As Celeste became anxious and closer to a meltdown, the need to wait added to the pressure as this is one thing she does not understand. It became harder for me to cope with my own distress. All sorts of questions were going through my mind. Was this going to become the norm? Was this necessary? Had I done something wrong? Why am I being questioned about my dog yet all the times my daughter has screamed the centre down, throwing her body around, hurling items and abusing me, not once has a security guard come to check whether she was alright and that I was not trying to kidnap or harm her. This did not make sense to me. As I sat I found myself in a situation of not knowing whether I should go to centre management to sort the issue out or to wait. Celeste feeds on my emotions. It is important I stay calm and level headed in order to keep her calm. With my mind whirring and ready to state the law if needed, the tension in my body built.

Just as I had made the decision to go to centre management to retrieve my identification the security guy came strolling across the courtyard with power in his step. As he handed me my identification, with no explanation or apology for the delay, he asked me if I had a letter from Smart Pups stating I was a trainer for them. I saw red. I had just given him an identification card which had photos and all the information on it that he needed. When I stated I did not have a letter as the identification was all that was required he again used his two way. The outcome of this was to inform me of the email address of centre management and ask me to forward a letter from Smart Pups prior to returning to the centre. Upon receiving this letter, centre management would make a decision as to whether Minnie could be trained at their centre. With this he stated I was permitted to continue my shopping for the day. This seemed ridiculous to me and I let the security guy know so. I explained to him that we had been shopping at this centre for years and that it was the centre I would be using once Minnie was certified. It was also the centre that was familiar to Celeste. It only made sense that this centre also became familiar to Minnie. As he turned to leave I grabbed my phone and, sitting right where I was, sent a quick email to Claire letting her know of the situation that had just unfolded. We continued our shopping that afternoon but it was not a pleasurable experience.

To their credit everyone at Smart Pups acted quickly, supporting us. Claire let me know she had forwarded my email to Patricia, who then promptly emailed me. Within her email she stated she could see a problem within our new program. Even when in training, assistance dogs and their puppy raisers are allowed to attend shopping centres but it is suggested they politely leave if asked, as puppies in training can get a little excited from time to time. With our program being a pilot program, where we are training an older dog who is a Greyhound, and Smart Pups are training the handler to train the dog, the ID card I was given would need amending. Upon stating this Patricia happily emailed the shopping centre advising them of the situation and the law. Within her email she pointed out the section of the Guide, Hearing and Assistance Dog act where it mentions dogs in training. Angela from centre management responded with an apology, stating that she appreciated Patricia's confirmation and that Minnie, Celeste and I were welcome back to the centre.

A few days later I visited the centre with first point of call being that of centre management where I asked to speak to Angela. I felt it necessary to meet Angela face to face and introduce her to Minnie and Celeste. This would give her the opportunity to ask any questions she may have and see that Minnie was a well behaved Greyhound. We had a lovely chat and I left feeling the incident was well behind us. How wrong I was.

Approximately a week later I returned to the centre for my weekly shopping trip. After being at the centre for approximately 10 mins I was approached by a security guard. As I saw him walking toward me I felt sick on the stomach but remained composed and smiling. I need not have worried about this guy as he approached cautiously and gently, briefly looking at Minnie's jacket. He stated he was told about the Greyhound service dog who visited the centre and wished me a lovely day. It seems a meeting had been held and all security guards were informed of Minnie.

We continued our journey along the main area of the shopping centre, crossing over into an outdoor section that took you from one wing to another. We had gone less than 25 metres when the trouble began again. Bounding towards me at a furious pace was a security guard with only negative business on his mind. He approached me with a roar in his voice asking me why I had the dog in the centre and was I authorised. I was taken aback but remained calm. In my bag was a printed copy of the email Angela had sent me, along with the law. I politely informed him that I had spoken to Angela at centre management who had given me permission to attend with Minnie. As I spoke I reached into my bag to pull out my paperwork. He was not going to have a bar of it. He continued to raise his voice, informing me that he was in charge of security not Angela and he needed to make the decision. As I stated the law he spoke over me, his voice booming down on me, suggesting I check the law again as he knew what it was and Minnie did not have the right badges on her coat. Keeping calm I let him know I would be speaking to Angela. He strongly suggested I leave the centre and shop elsewhere from now on. I was mortified. Passers-by were looking at us and people were stopping to see what was going on. Minnie, Celeste and I had been placed in an embarrassing and uncomfortable situation.

My first instinct was to get away from where I was. He turned to walk away so I took the chance to duck into the shop beside me for cover. It was here I found the toy aisle to keep Celeste quiet and I made a phone call. The call I made was to centre management in the hope of speaking to Angela. Unfortunately she was not in the office so I was put through to her message bank, leaving her a message to ring me as soon as possible as I was at the centre and a confrontation had occurred.

About 15 minutes later, while standing at the checkout at Target, Angela rang me. She was horrified at what she heard. She stated that the guy who approached me, Mark, was the operations manager and that he was aware of the last issue with Minnie. She apologised for any stress Mark may have caused and said that she would speak to him. We briefly discussed the law that Patricia had emailed to her and she asked if I could forward the information to her again. Upon arriving home I did so.

While walking around the shopping centre on that particular day we had at least three people who approached us stating they had seen the way we were approached and were appalled. They asked what the situation was about and said no one should be treated the way we were. I wish at the time I had thanked these people for their support more than I did but all I could do was hang my head in embarrassment, wanting to leave.

Two weeks later I had not heard from Angela in regards to the outcome of her discussion with Mark and whether Minnie was welcome at the centre. After sending her a polite email she responded with another apology, this time for her tardiness in reply, while explaining that she was only two months into the job of manager and was still working her way around the functioning of the centre. Again I was told that Minnie was welcome at the centre and should I be approached by staff to make sure I had my identification on hand and ask them to ring her. All that went through my mind was, "Yep, tried that one last time." Within the email she mentioned the centre's kids club and that they had sensory Santa at Christmas, saying they would like to welcome Celeste to join them. I felt the way she mentioned this was a little inappropriate at the time and a little too much on the marketing side for the situation.

I sent a reply along the lines of hoping that Mark had been spoken to about his behaviour and that maybe a few lessons on public relations would be a good idea for him. Angela suggested I drop in a copy of our identification card which she would place on the board in the office of security so all were aware of the right of Minnie to be in the centre.

While I was waiting two weeks for my response from Angela, Patricia was emailing Angela once again clarifying the law. It was at this time that Mark sent Patricia an email pushing his point that we do not have the right ID and that he suggests it is not a good idea to use a dangerous breed of dog as an assistance dog. What!!! Each time this guy opened his mouth he showed even more of his ignorance. Patricia's response was priceless: "Re your comments, Mark, I hardly think we would approve an aggressive or dangerous dog to be on our program and Minnie works with a 5 year old child, so I believe your customers are safe! Perhaps, if I may suggest, you hold a staff meeting, of which I would be happy to attend, where I can fully explain and educate all your security staff on the rights of an Assistance Dog... I appreciate your cooperation."

As days passed I was soon to learn that we were not the only victim of the centre's discrimination as the local media reported another incident where a Vietnam Vet who attended the centre with his assistance dog who helped him with PTSD was asked, on several occasions, to leave. Comments under the online news report in regards to this matter showed that there were enough assistance dogs who had been evicted from the centre for us to start our own little club.

A sour taste had been left in my mouth and it took some weeks before Celeste and I felt comfortable enough to attend the centre again. We entered with trepidation. Although our first time back went smoothly, it was not a comfortable experience. Still today, years later, this situation affects the way I feel each time I enter any shopping centre. To a degree it has scared us, leaving us entering all public places with Minnie awaiting to be approached and abused. People with disabilities and their assistance dogs should never be treated any differently from anyone else.

But they are....

# AND IT HAPPENS AGAIN AND AGAIN

We were soon to find out that the issue with the shopping centre was not to be the last. A couple of months later a blow came from an organisation who I would expect better from, the RSPCA at Wacol. This is an organisation who cares for stray animals, helping them find their forever home yet they showed a lack of understanding in regards to something which involved an animal that they profess to love.

It was a lovely warm day and we had decided to meet a friend at the RSPCA Black Cat Café. This café was attached to the shelter, giving visitors a chance to sit and relax, to have a chat after they had viewed the animals. I suppose they hope that the longer you sit there the harder it will be to resist those adorable animal eyes. The food is wholesome and healthy and the eatery, which provides a relaxed indoor and outdoor area is welcoming so it is the ideal place for us to meet friends. With Celeste's love of animals it is also a place where she feels calm. She could spend hours visiting the animals in need, giving me a well needed break while she is amused. Unfortunately on this occasion we were not welcomed nor did I receive a relaxed, well earned break.

When we arrived we walked from the carpark to the main foyer of the centre with Minnie in tow. The staff were all friendly, saying hello. They all looked at Minnie and said hello to her. We continued to walk through the main area, taking a wide birth around the cattery as although Minnie would not react we did not want to upset the cats. Walking into the café, my eyes scanned the place to find our friend had not yet arrived, after all we were five minutes early. I decided that I would approach the counter and order our food before finding a table. It was this decision that lead to our confrontation.

As I approached the counter a young lady who was collecting plates off the table nearby turned and yelled, "You need to get that dog out of here."

I was taken back, looking at her astounded. I calmly explained that Minnie was an assistance dog, pointing out the badges on her coat.

"I don't care what she is," was her response. "No dogs are allowed in the food area, not even our shelter dogs. You will have to take her outside to the tables out there."

With no other staff member coming to my aid I started to inform her of the law. All she was focussed on was that the dog had to leave. Not wanting to cause a scene, and realising this girl was not going to stop shouting, I took Minnie and Celeste and went out into the outdoor eatery. I found a table as far away from everyone else as I could and we sat and waited for our friend. I put Minnie into a down position next to the table and there she stayed the whole time we were at the café, not even flinching when rescue dogs walked by.

Prior to my friend arriving, I was stuck sitting at the table with Celeste rocking and having a meltdown as she wanted a drink. I was once again placed in a situation I should not have been in, one where Minnie was working hard to calm Celeste, with Celeste sitting on the ground and Minnie with her body on Celeste's legs, but the situation was out of control. Not one staff member came to ask if we were okay, as then I would have been able to mention that I could not get Celeste a drink as I could not take Minnie to the counter to order. Thankfully my friend arrived swiftly. I explained the situation to her and she proceeded to order our food and drink.

Our food was delivered to our table by an older lady who looked down at Minnie and then at me, taking it upon herself to thank me for bringing Minnie outside as dogs were not allowed in the café. I gave her a brief lesson on the Guide, Hearing and Assistance Dog Act, knowing it was a waste of my time. While doing so I made a mental note to email whoever was in charge and educate them. We didn't spend much time talking to the animals on this particular visit as all I wanted to do was get out of there.

Still not believing what had happened, I settled Celeste and Minnie with an activity when I got home and jumped online to contact the RSPCA. Finding an email address for administration I put together an email explaining the events that had unfolded. Included in my email was a snippet of the law.

> *Under the Act, a person with a disability who relies on a certified guide, hearing or assistance dog must have the same access rights as other members of the public. Further, they must not be segregated from other patrons or separated from their dog.*
>
> *Individuals in control of a public place or public transport vehicle can be fined up to $11,000.*
>
> *Privately owned businesses including restaurants, hotels, shops, taxis, theatres and sports facilities can be fined up to $55,000.*
>
> *These penalties commenced on 1 September 2009.*

I also wrote:

> *The behaviour by your staff member surprised me as the last place I would expect to be questioned and*

*asked to leave would be the RSPCA, a place where the welfare of animals and the placing of animals into caring homes is of utter importance, a place where awareness of all laws relating to animals, and such a basic one as the guide and assistance dog law, should be known. The RSPCA is a place that I thought would embrace the bond between animal and human and see worth in the therapy dogs offer to those with disability.*

My suggestion was that they should inform all their staff of the law so that the situation does not arise again. The following day I received a phone call from the manager of the RSPCA who was friendly, professional and apologetic. He said he had spoken to the staff involved and acknowledged that they were not aware of the law. He also admitted that he had never really given the law any thought and thanked me for bringing it to his attention. He said he had spent time looking into the law in full and would make sure it was on the agenda for the next staff meeting.

He was in damage control. On numerous occasions during our short conversation he asked for assurance that I would return to the Black Cat Café with Minnie and that I understood that we were always welcome. He asked me to approach the front desk next time I returned and ask to see him and he would shout us a meal, sitting with us to have a chat. We haven't ever gone back to the RSPCA. Not because we do not feel comfortable, I was very happy with the way the matter was handled by the manager, showing professionalism and care, but because time got away from us and we moved on in life.

Since this issue I have to say we have been pretty lucky. It was a good twelve months before we would again be met with any hostility. This was another shopping centre incident but was nowhere near as confrontational as the Ipswich issue.

We were sitting in the eatery at the shopping centre in Burleigh Heads on the Gold Coast. It seems we spend a lot of time at eateries. I was sitting with Alex and Celeste was interacting with the other kids in the play area. The table we were sitting at was next to the play equipment. Minnie was in a down position beside the table watching Celeste, ready to be given a command to help if needed. While enjoying our lunch I was approached by a security guard. I saw him coming, talking on his two way radio as the Ipswich guy had done, and my heart skipped a beat. I vaguely remember mumbling something along the lines of, 'Here we go again', to Alex.

We were approached calmly and gently which helped me relax a little but I still kept my guard up. I smiled at the guy and, after greeting him, let him know that Minnie was an assistance dog, yet again pointing out her badges. I was about to reach down for our ID when I was given a polite, 'Thank you, enjoy your day,' and the security guy was gone, but not for long...

He was soon back, and yes he was talking on his two way. He again approached me calmly, politely asking me to attend the manager's office each time I arrive at the centre and announce that I am here. I was told that this will just make things easier as all security will be told we are on the premises. As I looked at him all sorts of thoughts rushed through my mind. I thought about letting him know that under the law we have the same rights as other patrons. The discrimination act also quickly ran through my mind. By this stage I was tired of speaking up, tired of the uneducated and tired of fighting for my rights. This guy's saving grace was that he was polite and courteous. He had approached us in a way that showed he had some level of public relations understanding so I just nodded said, 'No problem,' and let him continue his day.

We have been back to that shopping centre on numerous occasions and not once have I visited centre management on arrival and not once have I been approached and questioned. I made the decision that the next staff member to approach me at that centre will not get off as lightly as the first security guy. I know it is only a matter of time before I am off to centre management introducing myself and having my say.

# OFF TO BOOT CAMP

It was not long after the issue at the shopping centre in Ipswich that it was decided that getting Minnie certified more quickly would make issues a lot easier to handle. Minnie was showing she was an extremely quick learner and it was felt that, with intensive training, she could be moved along more rapidly to certification. Because of the distance between the Sunshine Coast, where Smart Pups was located, and Ipswich, we were finding that there were gaps between formal training. Over the past week we had travelled to the Sunshine Coast for a mid week overnight stay, allowing Minnie to have two full days with Claire but the distance and commitments, as well as this being unsettling for Celeste, made more regular visits difficult. The cost was also a consideration. Although accommodation was covered by funding, my petrol and food were not. Even though I was always in contact with Claire via phone and email, and had Patricia as back up, Minnie's training was really the responsibility of Smart Pups. There was only so much I could do as an untrained handler and only so much Claire could teach me to teach Minnie. Claire and Smart Pups had years of expertise that I could never match.

I was doing well but there was still a lot Minnie needed to learn. All the trainers at Smart Pups had more than one dog in training at one time, and then there was the non-training time for placements of dogs with families that often saw them travelling interstate. After a lot of discussion and much consideration it was decided Claire and her co-trainer, Andrea, would take Minnie for two to three weeks of full-on boot camp training. It could take longer than this but that would be assessed closer to the two week mark.

The bond between Minnie and Celeste and the therapy Minnie was already providing needed to be taken into consideration. Claire and I discussed this and we then spoke to Celeste about what was going to happen. Minnie was going to have a short holiday at Claire's. Normally dogs are kennelled but in this situation Minnie would stay at Claire and Andrea's house. Claire felt this was best for Minnie as it would not undo the social interaction she was used to. We were sent daily reports and every few days Andrea would text Celeste photos of Minnie out and about. This gave Celeste something to look forward to and reinforced the fact that Minnie was on holiday.

We need not have worried about either Minnie or Celeste. They both took it in their stride. I must give Andrea credit for Celeste's ability to cope because without her constant feedback we would have been left wondering how Minnie was. Not a day went by that Celeste did not ask me numerous times what I thought Minnie was doing and if we had heard from Andrea.

Meanwhile Minnie was having the time of her life. Andrea and Claire had two other dogs and Minnie was enjoying playing with them when she was not working. Although she was not allowed in the house she had a comfy space in the garage where the other dogs lived. Although assistance dogs are part of the family they are working dogs first and foremost and this must be remembered at all times. For myself this means the free pats and being spoilt that my Labrador, Beauty, enjoys are given to Minnie only as a reward for acting on a command. This does not mean that assistance dogs are not loved as a 'pet' dog; they are probably actually loved and appreciated on a higher level. It just means that the affection and love comes at the price of a command. For Celeste, and others in the household, it is different, their love can come for free as it is me who Minnie must see as boss.

I was told that Claire and Andrea's garage was a doggy heaven as it came with all the creature comforts of a lounge and beds for each dog. It took a few days but Minnie soon claimed her sleeping spot and worked out that inside the house was out of bounds. Initially she would stand at the garage door that led into the house and look longingly at Andrea, even trying to squeeze past her from time to time. Andrea and Claire do not weaken when it comes to the dogs; standing firm and strong is part of the training process. Minnie had no option but to accept the fact that the garage was her place of abode.

When in training Minnie was the lady of the moment, out and about enjoying the events, markets and shopping that the Sunshine Coast has to offer. With each photo we were sent we could see the dedication and discipline etched in Minnie's face. Behind her beaming smile was a seriousness that glowed with a degree of pride.

At the end of the first week of boot camp I received this email from Claire:

> *Minnie is doing really well. I am confident that we can have her ready to hand over to you in two weeks. I was thinking the dates the 22nd – 23rd of July. I would bring Minnie down to you and complete her placement including her public access test over the two days. Then she will be your fully certified assistance dog (no more hassles from security guards).*
>
> *If you want to you are welcome to come up for a day of training next Thursday so you can practice handling skills which would make the placement the week after easier. It is up to you...*

*I have attached the handbook for you to read through so you can be across everything. Please study up on the motivation and reinforcement section.*

*Minnie is eating really well and has put on a small nice amount of weight. All the work is making her hungry!!!*

*I hope you are all doing okay without Minnie.*

If we want to visit next Thursday we can! Of course we want to! My reply to Claire was instant and within 24 hours we had arranged to meet on the Thursday at 8:30am. It was at this time that I realised I missed Minnie just as much as Celeste did, if not more. An 8:30am start on the Sunshine Coast would mean a 6:30am start from Ipswich but well worth it to see our special girl. I was concerned about how Celeste would cope with seeing Minnie and then having to leave her, and how Minnie would react to Celeste. What if she was no longer interested in Celeste? What if the bond had lessened? There was also the early start to the day which would mean a tired grumpy child by lunch time.

A few days after receiving the above email from Claire I received word that WIN News Sunshine Coast were interested in filming a segment on Minnie and Smart Pups. Would Celeste and I be willing to be part of the segment? Who could knock back the opportunity to support Smart Pups and bring attention to the training of Greyhounds as assistance dogs. The filming would take place on the Thursday morning while we were in attendance at the training grounds. Would Celeste be able to handle the filming and training all in one day, not to mention the trip in the car?

As the day drew closer I worried more. Not so much about seeing Minnie and the filming but about getting Celeste out the door early in the morning and coping with her and the long drive. I had mentioned the trip to Celeste after confirmation with Claire and she was excited, but I did not mention it after that as this would cause a week of anxiety which, by the time the day arrived, would make the day itself one that we were all unable to cope with.

The afternoon prior to the morning of our travel I mentioned that we would have to rise early the next day as we were going on a long drive to see Minnie, making sure she was clear that Minnie was not coming home with us. Her face lit up and she started bouncing around the room. The excitement set in immediately with her planning what toys she was taking. Celeste never left the house, even to go to the corner shop, without a variety of toys. I tried explaining to her that toys were not necessary when we were going to buy milk but this just escalated the anxiety that was already in place. Then there was the anxiety about taking her toys into the shop and being able to carry them. What if she lost them and so on and so on. Over the years I had created a lot of tactics which I put into place depending on the situation. These were used to convince her to take only a few toys and that they would be fine if left in the car. Convincing her not to take any was something I knew she would never cope with. My tactics did not always work and I needed to create new ones on a regular basis but I did my best. Being a mother of a child with Autism means getting creative with the way you handle situations, constantly trying to stay a step ahead of the meltdowns. All one could ever really do was ride the waves. The more I spoke the more I filled her mind with words that confused her. It takes a degree of skill to know when to speak and when to be quiet. More often than not I get it wrong and am screamed at, told I am an idiot and I'm ducking as items are hurled at me.

With the toys for the big day out being placed in a bag at the front door so that we would not forget them, I endeavoured to put Celeste to bed early. At this stage she was still sleeping in the double bed with me as she could not bear to be in a room by herself, even when asleep. The night tremors were also easier to cope with if she was in the same room as me. The Risperidone had lessened these episodes but they were still regular. Putting Celeste to bed involved a bedtime story and then I had to lie in bed with her, with the lights out, until she was asleep. I could then either get up, if there were things I needed to do, and continue my night or turn the bedside light on and read. Most nights I chose to read as I was already snug and saw no sense is getting up. I had a television in my room but found that I had little time or patience for regular prime time viewing. My iPad has become a friend of mine over the years, allowing me to write while sitting up in bed. I had a desktop computer but finances did not allow me to purchase a laptop so a keyboard compatible to the Ipad was my solution. On this particular night I put Celeste to bed at 7.00pm, one hour earlier than usual. With her not being able to tell the time, getting her to bed early, especially when she is tired, is easy. Yes I am guilty of telling her it is 8:00pm and bedtime even though it isn't.

Early to bed was not to be on this night. The excitement was too great and could only lead to anxiety. The normal routine of book was adhered to, with an extra book or two being thrown in when it was obvious one was not working. By 10:00pm I was at boiling point. Celeste was talking incessantly, something she does when she is anxious, worrying about every fine detail of the trip. How long would it take? Would it still be dark when we left? Would Minnie be excited to see us? Where were we meeting Claire? What if we were late?....

My head was spinning and my shoulders were tense. Was this child ever going to shut up and go to sleep? By 10:30pm I was reaching for the Nurofen which is called upon to calm Celeste when the anxiety is not only too much for her but too much for me. 10:45pm saw peace and quiet. Finally she was snoring soundly. I was exhausted and ready to pass out myself.

Why do the hours pass so quickly when you are asleep? Not being an early riser, 5:00am, and still dark, was not a favourable time to me. Showered, dressed and coffee in hand I sat and contemplated how, in the next 30 minutes or so, I was going to wake a sleeping child without too much fuss. I really need not have worried. On this occasion my anxiety seemed to be much higher than hers.

I decided the best way to attack the situation was to place everything in the car, including a change of clothing for Celeste, and then gently pick her up and place her in her seat in a half asleep state. I hoped she might doze off and then the first half of the journey would be quiet for Alex and I. As I picked her up I spoke to her softly letting her know that I was putting her in the car and reassuring her that all of her toys were waiting for her. I carried her down the stairs to the car wrapped in a blanket, as the chill leading up to winter was apparent. As her bum hit the seat she sprang to life as if she had been awake for hours. First thing was to feel the seat beside her for her toys, all accounted for and then the chatter started. Meltdown had been diverted. After a small diversion to the drive thru at McDonalds where breakfast was hash browns, English muffins with jam, juice, and another coffee for Mummy, I was confident we would get half our trip in before we needed to stop. The focus was naturally on Minnie. What was she doing now? Did I think she knew we were coming? Would she be there on time? Did I know where we were meeting her?

Stopping halfway at a service station gave me a chance to quickly dress Celeste. This was easier than expected as I was able to use looking good for Minnie to encourage her.

A quick cool drink for Celeste and Alex and another coffee for Mum and we set off on the second leg of our journey. Music kept us occupied as we sang the hour away.

We once again met Claire at Buderim for a hard day of training, not really of Minnie but of myself. A shady spot was found under a tree where a picnic blanket and Celeste's toys were placed. Alex sat with her as they both watched Minnie show me what she could do. The training ground was abuzz with dogs and trainers, not only doing their thing but ready to be part of the filming with WIN News if needed. There was an hour or so before the arrival of the news crew so Claire was able to run us through what Minnie had learnt over the past week. The change in Minnie's ability was amazing. All commands, when given by Claire, were acted upon immediately. When given by me, well, that was another story. Minnie was a lot slower in her response and at times a little confused, not due to anything that was her fault but due to my newness at giving the commands in the correct manner. Claire was lovely, reinforcing that I was grasping it all really quickly and that it would become easier as time went by. Apparently after a week or so of having Minnie full time it would all be second nature. I doubted it at the time but of course Claire was right.

The news crew arrived mid morning and filming went smoothly. There were giggles as attaching a GoPro camera to Minnie's training coat was attempted. With this came Minnie bucking like a rodeo bull as she felt the weight of the GoPro on her coat. The attempt to secure footage of an assistance dog from a dog's eye view failed but the rest of the report went well. Minnie behaved in true Minnie style and Celeste was a true superstar. I was interviewed and asked all the normal questions reporters ask such as what was life like prior to Minnie and how had it changed. There were the questions concerning how all this came about and what Smart Pups meant to us. There were no nerves on my part, being used to public speaking, with Patricia commenting that she could see I had done this sort of thing before. When aired, the report was well received with the Sunshine Coast Daily Newspaper running a written story.

With the filming over, lunchtime was soon upon us. We left Minnie with Claire so she could have a well earned rest and set off to the local shops for a bite to eat. Having only been to the area once before I was a little unsure about where I was going but confident I could find my way. All went well and we soon found ourselves in the heart of Maleny. With Red Rooster in front of us we found parking and took our hungry tummies to a table to eat. Finding food to eat seemed to be the easy part, finding our way back to the dog training park was what seemed to be the challenge. Somehow, somewhere I took a wrong turn. Why, when this happens does one get flustered and take even more wrong turns? As I have a GPS, I don't know how I still manage to get lost, but I do. As the GPS yelled at me telling me to redirect, Celeste freaked out. What if we never found our way back? What if we were lost forever? I yelled at the GPS and the situation got a little out of control. Eventually, with a lot of deep breaths, we all refocussed and we are back with Celeste and Minnie having a calming cuddle. As always, I arrived at my destination joking to Claire about getting lost, seeing the funny side of life.

The afternoon went well. Before we left, Claire had a treat for Celeste. She had taught Minnie how to do some little tricks that brightened Celeste's day. These were tricks that Celeste could do with Minnie encouraging bonding and fun times. Minnie could now shake hands with Celeste and give her a high five, along with choosing which closed hand Celeste had a treat in by pawing at the hand when asked 'which hand'. Such simple little things made Celeste giggle and gave her ownership of some of the training.

During our time working with Smart Pups it was wonderful to work with a team who truly understood Autism, who understood that each child is different and asked all the right questions so that each dog was trained to meet the needs of the individual child and family. Smart Pups not only listens but they understand and they care. The staff are gentle, kind, caring and patient. During the training of Minnie no question was a stupid question. If I didn't understand something or I struggled to get the command right I was given the attention and time I needed. Their training of their dogs is the same. At no time is the dog reprimanded for anything or treated with disrespect. Training is done using a reward program that offers gentle persuasion and lots of cuddles. It is important that, at all times, the dogs in training enjoy what they are doing and the trainers they are with. Smart Pups understand that each dog, like each child and family, is an individual. Introducing their dogs to the Smart Pups program as a pup, time is then spent getting to know the personality of each dog. They understand that it may take one dog a little longer to achieve a command than another and that some may not be suitable for the job. As the pups grow and progress through the program they are matched with a family and taught the necessary skills needed to assist the child they are assigned to. No dog, or family, is ever placed so far out of their comfort zone that they feel threatened.

Our day with Minnie come to a close with a huge cuddle and a promise we would see her soon. We said goodbye to our girl and started our long drive home. Even Alex, who was not a dog person, embraced Minnie, telling her he was proud of her. I was sure Celeste would sleep on the drive home but fuelled with the excitement of her day, and the junk food she had consumed, she chatted away madly about Minnie and her tricks. We all felt we couldn't wait for

Minnie to be back with us full time but knew that she was happy, safe and having the time of her life in the loving care of Smart Pups.

While all this was happening, our Smart Pup for Celeste Facebook page was being bombarded with photos of Greyhounds. Celeste looked forward to the photos, asking me regularly throughout the day if there were any new ones. She viewed each and every photo, with myself typing a message on her behalf. She marvelled at the different colours, names and sizes. Through Minnie she was connecting to others and socialising online.

# A LITTLE TEST...

Over the next two weeks the positive feedback from Claire and Andrea on Minnie's training continued. Each day we got closer and closer to Minnie's return and certification. On 22nd July, one week prior to my birthday, Claire arrived at our home with Minnie and the paperwork that would move us into the next chapter of our lives.

Over the period of training Minnie I had found that Claire and I had a lot of common interests and related well. There was time for a drink, something to eat and a chat prior to doing the paperwork and certification. When Claire arrived I was feeling a little nervous as not only was Minnie doing her public access test but I was doing my handler testing. Claire quickly put my nerves at ease with her friendly disposition and a chat about life. By the time she left I felt as though I had found a new friend who understood my life. While chatting, we attended to business of course. We went over the paperwork that had to be filled in and discussed the process of the testing. Claire had brought Minnie her official service dog coat, as her previous coat had 'in training' on it. The coats come plain, so time was spent sewing the patch that said 'service dog' onto the coat, along with the Guide, Hearing and Assistance dog badge and the Smart Pups logo. We were all prepared for Minnie to pass her test; if she did not, then the coat was ready for when she did.

The testing was to take place at the shopping centre where we had experienced so much difficulty earlier. It was decided that this was the best place as it was the one we visited most frequently, giving me the opportunity to iron out any issues

I may find I had and to ask questions while Claire was present. Claire jumped in her car, as she would leave directly from the centre after testing, and I drove mine with Celeste and Minnie. It was a nice feeling having Minnie back in her spot on the seat. It was decided that when we arrived at the shopping centre we would go directly to centre management and see Angela. This would allow Angela to meet a Smart Pups representative face to face and give us a chance to let her know that Minnie was to become a certified assistance dog under the Guide, Hearing and Assistance Dog law. At the time it was a decision made solely for the reasons of making peace with the past issue and being polite but now I look back at it I suppose we were rubbing it in Angela's face slightly. We were giving her a polite warning that as a certified team we had legal rights.. The law was the law and we had worked hard to earn our right to public access.

Our arrival at centre management was a welcoming one from the moment we approached the front desk asking for Angela up until the moment we had spoken to Angela and left. We felt we could finally put the past behind us and that, with any luck, all staff at the centre were now aware of the law.

With formality behind us we were ready to move on to the reason we were there in the first place, the public access test. Feeling apprehensive about my ability to give Minnie the commands and have her follow them, the nerves set in. Claire stayed cool and calm. After all it wasn't she who was being tested. She explained that we would just take Minnie for a walk around the centre and she would instruct me to give commands as we went along. Minnie took it all in her stride. It seemed nothing upset this dog. She was miss cool, calm and collected in all situations.

As we walked the chatting remained general causing me to soon forget that Minnie and I were being tested. The clipboard and pen Claire held and the occasional marking off of points on her piece of paper became oblivious to me. Celeste walked along beside us enjoying the chatting and the strokes of Minnie's soft coat that kept her calm.

We tackled the travelators, stairs and lift with no trouble. When given the command to sit or go into a down, Minnie reacted instantly. We purchased a drink in the eatery section where I was told to ask Minnie to place herself in a down position close to the table where she would not hinder other customers. This is a little more difficult for a Greyhound than it is for a Labrador or Retriever as a Greyhound's body structure and long legs don't enable it to curl up under a table or chair out of the way. Allowances are made for this with the main focus being on Minnie being in a position where she will not cause someone to trip or where she will be trodden on. Greyhounds do not fold their legs under themselves like other dogs do when they sit. For Minnie to sit, she 'squats' with her bottom elevated from the ground. This position cannot be held for any lengthy period. If I know Minnie will be asked to stay in a sit position for a period of time she will be placed in the down position. When going into a down, she 'sits' first by placing her hip on the ground and then she slides her front paws down in front of her. After being in this position for some time, when she realises we will be staying in the one spot, she will lie down on her side with her legs sprawled out in front of her. Greys grab every opportunity they can to lie down and sleep. This lying down is where the tripping hazard arises. Consideration needs to be given to the time frame when I place Minnie in a down position and ask her to stay there. If this time period extends for longer than I anticipated, I need to reposition her in order to avoid a hazard. At the time of testing it was known that the period of time would be short so the down position right next to the table, between our chairs and the next table, was appropriate. Minnie was not in the way of foot traffic.

Next we moved on to achieving the wait command. We found an area near the escalators that was large enough for me to place Minnie in a down, tell her to wait, let go of her lead and walk away. This was a true test of her ability as Greys are known for taking the opportunity to run once they feel the lead is free and the space is open. This was my big concern during the whole training process and a characteristic of Greys that I had discussed with Claire over and over. It worried me and I tended to panic a little. Once again I need not have panicked. Minnie listened and she stayed. The moment I called her to come she was at my heels. Today she is still as obedient as ever. When taken for a run at an off-lead dog park she is always listening to command and returns the minute I call her to come. Of course she is allowed to run as she feels free in a dog park. This is her time to let off steam, and time for Celeste to let off steam with her. For Minnie life is about pleasing her master and being there for Celeste. She is truly disciplined and dedicated. I often wish I had her discipline and dedication, along with her muscley thighs.

From sit and wait to leave it. The aisles of Woolworths became our next destination. Here Minnie was put through the test of walking through the meat section without reacting to the smell. She needed to stay focussed on her job of helping Celeste at all times and be ready for my command. She didn't bat an eyelid. Claire walked ahead of us placing treats in a row on the ground. As we approached them I gave Minnie the leave it command, having her walk over the treats without being tempted to eat them. Achieve, achieve, achieve was all that Minnie knew how to do.

Testing was quick but intensive. There was testing on how I reacted when someone approached me and went to pat my dog. Minnie was tested on her reaction when a stranger approached her, waving things in her face and touching her. Her reaction to a loud sudden noise was tested at which she looked but did not jump or attempt to run.

We passed! Minnie had done it. She had gone from racetrack to assistance dog in less than a year. She was officially the first Greyhound to become a Smart Pup Assistance Dog. We were over the moon. Our journey as a family had officially started. There was no more concern that Minnie would fail and decisions would need to be made as to what journey her life would then take. Her life journey was that of an assistance dog.

Our life as a three part team was official.

# MINNIE MEETS TODD MCKENNEY

Timing of certification could not have been better as my birthday, seven days later, saw us going to the musical 'Anything Goes' starring Todd McKenney. Sam arrived from South Australia a few days beforehand and we went as a family. Minnie could now attend as a certified part of the family instead of being an assistance dog in training. Todd was yet to meet Minnie so it was an exciting day for us all. We had arranged to meet Todd after the show.

'Anything Goes' was on at the Queensland Performing Arts Centre (QPAC) which was located in Brisbane, a 45 minute drive from Ipswich. I booked matinee tickets as I felt this would be easier for Celeste. Being new at this assistance dog thing I gave no thought to taking Minnie when I booked. Approximately a month prior to the day I emailed QPAC letting them know that I would be bringing an assistance dog, hoping that there would be no dramas. Dramas there were not, it was exactly the opposite. The staff at QPAC fell over backwards for us, making sure we were comfortable and that Celeste enjoyed every moment of her theatre experience. They are well educated on Autism and special needs, often holding special sessions of shows to accommodate people with special needs. We were in good hands.

Soon after sending my email I received a phone call from a lovely lady at QPAC who said she had looked at my seats which were two rows from the stage and did not feel they were appropriate due to the noise and lighting. I had not given this any thought as, although I had been to the theatre many times, I was not familiar with all aspects of it. At the time of booking all that was on my mind was getting good seats where we could see what was going on. It was soon pointed out to me that it is a misconception that the seats up the front are the best. Apparently any regular and serious theatre goer knows that these seats are not the best, with your view often obstructed and the noise level high. You are also unable to see the whole stage, missing the action at the back. We were invited to visit QPAC to look at the theatre prior to the show. This would allow us to view the seats we had and discuss what else might be more suitable. Celeste and Alex would also be able to see the theatre in its empty capacity, familiarising themselves with the surroundings and the darkness. This would lessen the anxiety leading up to and on the day.

The following week Alex, Celeste and I drove into Brisbane, making it a day out for lunch, and had our tour. This, of course, included Minnie. We were shown our seats, which, we all agreed were wrong for us due to location, and we were given alternative options. There were spaces allocated for wheelchairs and disabled patrons which at the time had no seats but these could be added. This spot was perfect. Even with the seats in place it was spacious and near an exit should I need to vacate quickly with Celeste. Just outside the exit was the quiet room. This was a soundproof room that we were welcome to use should we need it. An usher would be more than happy to escort us. The room had a large glass front so that the stage could still be seen but being sound proof any noise made would not annoy others. The sound from the stage that filtered into the room was also of a lower volume than that outside. I was instantly in love with QPAC. To have this service available to patrons, to cater for special needs and to understand Autism put them high on my list of places I would visit regularly. I now knew that regardless of how Celeste was on the day, our theatre experience it going to be a good one. My birthday was going to be fantastic. The following week I received tickets for our new seating, along with a refund in my account as the price of the new tickets was less than I had originally paid.

I looked forward to the event as going out anywhere with Celeste was difficult and something such as this was a mammoth event. Being a single mum with no family in Queensland also limited me to what I could do as wherever I went Celeste always went too. With one income in the house and the responsibilities of all finances being on my shoulders, it was rare that I had the cash flow allowing me to attend such an event. This surely was a splurge and to have my three children attend, and Minnie, as a family, was magical.

To make the event even more special and to give Celeste the full experience of a special occasion we dipped further into the funds and went shopping, purchasing a new outfit for both of us to wear. It wasn't anything flash or expensive but it was new and a shopping experience we shared together. It occurred to me while in the dressing room trying on outfits that it was the first time in the life of Celeste that I had actually been able to try on clothes in a calm manner, without Celeste running in and out of the dressing room or lying on the floor and rocking. As I tried on a few dresses Celeste lay on the floor of the dressing room next to Minnie cuddling her and stroking her. She was calm, not even saying a word. I was astounded. The tears of happiness started to run down my face. I finally felt as though I might be able to achieve some of the little things that other mums can do. I spoke quietly to Celeste asking her opinion on outfits as I tried them on but she said little. She just sat with Minnie and stroked her. A few days into having Minnie as a fully certified assistance dog and my world was changing. One small thing meant so much to me. I think about it now and realise that I still rushed trying the clothes on, getting in and out as quickly as possible, but while rushing I was not tearing my hair out, worried about judgement due to a screaming child and not carrying a heavy weight on my shoulders. When I had tried on the last dress, I gave Minnie the let's go command and, as she stood, so did Celeste. I gave them both a huge hug thanking them for letting me try on clothes and for being so beautiful. It took a lot to compose myself and not punch the air and shout 'yes'. I am sure people were wondering why the smile on my face was so huge when I left the dressing room. I bought one of the dresses I had tried on, the first decent dress I had purchased in many years, and today it is still one of my favourites. Not because it is an overly wonderful dress but because of the memories it holds.

The day arrived and we were all excited. We had picked Sam up from the airport a few days earlier so had already started our little celebration, although this only consisted of a few hours out to grab a coffee, the rest being at home with Celeste enjoying the company of her sister in a familiar meltdown-lessening environment. When Sam visited Celeste loved to do 'girly' things with her such as hair and looking pretty. This love of hair and 'girly' things made the morning of 'Anything Goes' a little smoother. There were the normal getting ready meltdowns and the new clothes I had purchased as a special treat soon created a huge anxiety attack as Celeste had not worn them before. As far as a sensory experience went, they were an overload. They felt different, sat on her body differently, smelt different and were not the clothes she wore every day. The new shoes we had bought were abandoned for the dirty, ugly sandals but all this did not matter. Her hair looked pretty as she let her sister style it. At the end of the day all that mattered was that she was comfortable in not only how she felt but in how she looked. There was still anxiety while in the car driving to Brisbane. This was not only due to the uncertainty of what was happening next but due to her feeling that she had failed herself by not being able to wear her new outfit. Nothing is ever simple when Autism and anxiety are in your life. Minnie was there for Celeste to ease the meltdown, lying her body across Celeste, offering comforting pressure and reassurance while Celeste stroked her, but she could not take away the feelings of disappointment Celeste had in herself or the voices which spoke in her head, telling her she had let everyone down.

We arrived at the QPAC and parked the car, walking down to the theatre with plenty of time to spare before the show started. As we were walking down the main external foyer that ran from the main road down to the cultural precinct and South Bank we could see a male walking towards us. It took a moment for me to realise that he was calling Minnie and Celeste's names as he quickened his pace towards us. This man was the one and only Todd McKenney, walking up to start a day at work.

I don't know who was more excited, my family or Todd. Hugs were exchanged all round, with the humans naturally having to wait a while for their hug as the embrace of Minnie came first and foremost and was the longest. It is no secret that Todd loves Greyhounds and misses his dearly when he is away from home. His excitement over seeing Minnie and getting to give love to a Grey was infectious. I was pleased to finally be able to thank him face to face for all he had done to help bring Minnie into our lives and all the support he had continued to offer. Taking the back seat to a hug with Minnie was the least I could do. Of course Minnie had no idea who this man was but she leaned into him, lapping up the full embrace in true Greyhound style. As Todd enjoyed his cuddles he just kept telling her how beautiful and how petite she was. He couldn't get over her small size, saying she was a perfect little package, just right for the job. Celeste also loved the attention she got from Todd as he spoke to her about her special dog. In just that brief moment Todd was touching Celeste's life more than he realised. She was captivated by him, soaking in his positive and exuberant personality. His experience with children with Autism and his compassion shone through. Before I even had a chance to ask Todd if we could get photos of him with Minnie and Celeste he had his camera in his hand and was asking Sam if she could take some photos for him. Handing his camera over, he stayed in the squatted position at eye level with Celeste and smiled. As Todd saw me pull my camera out he held his pose, looking in my direction. This photo really is priceless.

Here was a man who had saved the life of a Greyhound, through his own generosity and love, with a little girl who was finding her place in this world with her new found assistance dog. This was a bond between the three of them that would last forever.

Todd was due in makeup so our chat was cut short but it was full of jovial chatter, zest for life, and lots of laughter. It was as though we had always known him. We arranged to chat more after the show.

With time still to spare we continued our walk into the South Bank promenade where we found a café that suited our taste, although Celeste found the music a little loud which had me wondering how she was going to cope in the theatre. We ate a lovely lunch, taking the time to bond as a family. As it grew closer to showtime we made our way back to the theatre. As we walked along the promenade there was a man busking, his beautiful operatic voice travelling through the air. It was Celeste who pointed out that he was Tim McCallum who she had been barracking for on The Voice not so many weeks ago. Tim was in a wheelchair after a diving accident had left him a quadriplegic. Celeste asked me if she could have some money to give to him. As Celeste approached Tim finished the song he was singing, smiling at Celeste like a true gentleman, thanking her for the kind donation. As Celeste's face lit up Tim noticed Minnie, mentioning he had an assistance dog at home named Roxy. It was a brief but touching moment between the two, one that Celeste will never forget as she locked eyes with a man whose voice she had idolised through a television screen. The common bond of an assistance dog fuelled her flame. Here was a little girl who only weeks ago would not approach anyone or make eye contact yet with Minnie to hold onto she was tackling socialisation head on. Minnie was the social ice breaker which gave her a feeling of others being interested in her, boosting her self worth.

Our seats in the theatre were just as perfect as I had visualised. Celeste and I sat on the end so we could make a quick getaway with Minnie lying on the floor in front of us. I had purchased a program prior to the show, spending time looking at it with Celeste before the show started, keeping her amused and giving her further understanding of what to expect. As the lights dimmed Celeste leant into me grabbing my arm but as the sound started it sparked her interest and her hesitation was soon forgotten. This was not to be for long as no more than 5 minutes into the show she was down on the floor with her hands over her ears cuddling Minnie, who, as always, was taking it in her stride. Celeste soon noticed that Minnie was okay with the sound and stood up to tell me that Minnie liked the music. With this she sat back on her seat and watched for a while. Not being able to sit still for long periods, she soon became agitated, saying she wanted to go outside and that she needed a drink. Between watching the show I cuddled her, encouraged her to cuddle Minnie and told her that it would be intermission soon and then I would get her an ice cream and drink.

Saved by intermission, we made an exit to the main foyer. A toilet visit and the promised drink and ice cream saw us ready to enter the theatre for the second half of the show.

I could tell going into the show that Celeste was tense and struggling. Trying to keep her calm I discussed the first half of the show with her, asking her about the costumes and discussing how clever the actors were. Having met Todd he was my drawcard for distraction as she could relate the conversation to the person she had just been speaking to. I made a point of mentioning how well Minnie was behaving, asking Celeste what part of the show she thought Minnie would have loved so far. As the lights dimmed she was a little more relaxed but obviously not enough. The early stages of a meltdown soon began. Her talking became repetitive and agitated. She jumped around from sitting on the floor with Minnie to standing in front of her seat, annoying the people in front of us. As the headbanging started I knew it was time to get her out of there. At all times while we were in the theatre there was an usher right next to us ready to lend me a hand. The minute I stood with Minnie and started guiding Celeste toward the door the usher was there asking me if I was okay. He opened the first exit door and helped me into the area between this door and the next. By this stage it was impossible to get Celeste to go any further as she fell onto the floor in a heap. All I could do was give Minnie the lap command and speak quietly to Celeste letting her know it was okay. The usher calmly asked me if there was anything he could do. I thanked him and let him know that we were okay, Celeste just needed a minute. The quiet room was offered but I declined as at this stage I did not wish to fill Celeste's head with any offers or to change her environment any further. The usher stayed with me but stood at a distance in the dark corner near the door leading into the theatre. It was comforting to know that someone, even a stranger, was there for me.

The corridor we stood in was dim and cool and although the sound of the stage could be heard it was at a peaceful level. This was enough for Celeste to calm so that I could reassure her and listen to how she was feeling. We both sat on the floor against the wall, with Minnie's head on Celeste's lap as we stroked her ear and forehead. We didn't say a lot. We just sat, stroked and listened to what was happening on the stage. Not only was Minnie offering a safe haven and peaceful moment to Celeste but she was providing this to me also. During this moment Minnie was the common bond between Celeste and myself. She was our connection. This would be found to be the case on many occasions.

When Celeste was ready we all rose and the usher helped us return to our seats. The rest of the show was enjoyed by Celeste. A meltdown is often what is needed to bring Celeste around so she can enjoy an event. Meltdowns are her way of releasing the tension and making sense of her world. Unfortunately these meltdowns come at the final stages of a day out, meaning that Celeste only gets to enjoy a small part of the end of the day. It never ceases to amaze me though, how much of the events that are happening during Celeste's anxiety and meltdown she can recall and speak of in detail. It seems that externally she is fixated and controlled by her meltdown but internally she is interacting with the world around her. During her meltdown period, and leading up to it, I lose far more acknowledgment and interaction mentally with my surroundings than she does. I often wonder if I have the meltdown thing all wrong. To me it seems a stressful and difficult thing to cope with, looking physically and emotionally painful. My heart bleeds for Celeste as I watch her confused face and her hurtful actions, but maybe I am wrong. Maybe it is this way externally, but internally it is just what her body, her mind, needs to do in order to make sense of the situation and the world around her. Stimming is a sense of relief and I suppose meltdowns are also but in a cruel, confusing and loud way that is socially unacceptable. The autistic mind will always remain a mystery to me.

After the show we headed back to the stage door to meet with Todd. It didn't take long before he was walking out the door asking us how we liked the show and yet again embracing Minnie. Being a very busy man this was again a brief meeting but it was not the end of our chats or the last time we would see each other.

During our lunch prior to the show we had noticed a food festival that was being held on the grass area just outside the QPAC. We decided that we would head in that direction as this provided a place for Minnie to toilet and have a drink and there was plenty of space for Celeste to run. We could also grab some dinner before we headed back to Ipswich. However, our walk through this area was brief as Celeste was tired and pushed to her limit so we felt the best thing to do was go home. Before we left we grabbed some Asian food to eat on the run.

The day ended peacefully. Our drive home went smoothly, with our Labrador, Beauty, pleased to see us and Minnie after a day at home by herself. My concerns about Beauty feeling left out as Minnie went everywhere with us were not warranted. The two dogs quickly worked out their roles in the family.

# THE DOORS OPEN TO MANY OPPORTUNITIES...

As time passed my dreams of Celeste being able to get out and about and engage in the activities of that of her peers began to come true. Minnie was all I dreamed of and more. With Minnie came opportunities we would not otherwise have had. Things were still hard. The Autism and anxiety did not just miraculously disappear nor did the learning difficulties or the auditory processing disorder fix themselves. What did happen was the improvement in the ability to go out. We still have meltdowns that mean it takes us longer than a 'normal' family to get out the front door but these meltdowns lessened in length due to Minnie being by Celeste's side. With Minnie beside her, Celeste has gained confidence in her ability to walk through a shopping centre or to look at others and smile. If someone speaks to her, or she wants to speak to them, Minnie is always there as the topic of conversation. When out and about with an assistance dog you cannot hide; everyone notices you, looks and comments. When your assistance dog is a Greyhound, a breed which is being mentioned in the media on a daily basis and is going through such hardship, others show an interest. People stop and chat. They want to know more. This could have gone two ways: Celeste could have hated it and it could have created a bubble of anxiety or she could have embraced it and thrived on the attention. The latter was the outcome.

Facebook has been a great support and asset to Celeste whilst travelling the Minnie journey. The internet is her major learning device, her security and her obsession. Facebook has allowed her to take this obsession and tap into the world of others. It is hard to really put into words the appreciation of the support, friendship and acceptance of our Facebook family. With each like of a status, each photo of a Greyhound shared to our page and each comment, Celeste blossoms. She notices words and letters, she asks me to read what people post, she asks me to take photos to share and, most of all, she connects with society on a level I never thought I would ever see.

From time to time we get to meet a Facebook friend in real life as we run into them at shopping centres or at events. We love it when people introduce themselves letting us know they follow us on Facebook. This is a beautiful connection with another person that would not be possible had Minnie not come into our lives. This connection takes the online friendship to a new level, enhancing the overall socialisation experience for Celeste. An example of this is our Facebook friend, Sue, who lives nearby and works at the local Coles which we visit each week. One day, as we were walking up and down the aisles in Coles, a face popped out from behind a cash register, waved and shouted out to Celeste and Minnie. We had no idea who this beautiful soul was but she made us smile. By the time we had filled our trolley and worked our way back toward the checkout this face had disappeared. Feeling sad I updated our Facebook status hoping the person would reveal themselves. Sue soon popped up. Hooray! We now had a name to the face. From that day on Celeste has loved going to Coles. She goes to see Sue and have a chat. She eagerly searches the checkouts looking for her and is sad if she is not there. As Sue rings up our groceries Celeste chats to her, sharing the toys she brought with her, conversations about Minnie and the purchases she has made during the trip. Sue has become part of Celeste's life, enriching it and offering not only memories but a chance to develop skills she might not have previously developed. Still today she talks of the time Sue let her scan her KinderEgg.

When Minnie came into our lives we also became part of the Greyhound community, a community which spreads far and wide. There is something about dog people that is special. Within the Greyhound community there is a special bond that only those who own a Greyhound truly understand. From the day we first started to search for Minnie we were enveloped in their love and support. When Minnie came into our lives via Greyhounds New Beginnings we instantly became part of their family. Over time we have been given the opportunity to support them and return the love by attending fundraiser BBQ's and parties. You can always be guaranteed a day of fun, acceptance and non-judgement support with your Grey. For Celeste these events offer an opportunity of normality. The common bond of her Greyhound allows her to feel accepted by the other children and gives her a common ground to start conversation. She is quick to tell her peers that her Greyhound is special as she helps her with her Autism. Minnie has provided Celeste with an acceptance of the fact that she has Autism and finds it harder than her peers to do some things but that is okay, she is special as she has Minnie. This feeling, and the support of Minnie, gives her the strength to cope when she is questioned about being different or if she is bullied. We have experienced many situations, none within the Greyhound group, where Celeste is singled out and bullied by other children, who can be cruel when they come across a child who just does not seem right. With Minnie leaning on her, Celeste stands strong, pats Minnie, talks to her and lets Minnie know that the children are nasty and that she will find someone else to play with.

In my role as a literary publicist I have many opportunities to attend book events, meeting authors from all walks of life. One of these opportunities that will always remain clear in the minds of Celeste and myself is meeting of Tim and Judy Sharp. Tim is an adult cartoonist who is known for his character Laser Beak Man. Tim has Autism but this has not stopped him, with the support of his mum, from taking Laser Beak Man around the world. In her book 'A Double Shot of Happiness', Judy Sharp speaks of the trials and tribulations of being the mum of an autistic child. As I read her words I related to them. I cried tears of sadness and tears of joy. I felt despair but I also felt hope for my own family. After reading the book I knew that other parents needed to hear what Judy and Tim had to say. I set about contacting Judy asking her if she would come and speak to the local Ipswich Autism Spectrum Disorder parents group. She politely accepted my invitation. The next few weeks were spent organising the event.

My admiration for Judy and Tim only increased. To hear Judy speak publicly of her struggles as the single mum of a child with Autism and to meet Tim, an adult who was coping within society, touched all who attended the event. For Celeste this was the first time she had met an adult who she was aware had Autism. She listened to Tim's achievements and viewed his art work with awe. In her eyes Tim was very clever. She fully appreciated the humour behind Laser Beak man from the point of view of an autistic mind. She sat with Minnie, taking in every slide Judy showed and listening to Tim as he answered Judy's questions and spoke about a few of his drawings. Minnie was an angel. She sat on the floor next to Celeste's seat and did not move a muscle. For her this was a great opportunity to catch up on some Greyhound siesta time. Again Minnie broke the ice when Celeste wanted to approach Tim. Tim asked about Minnie and Celeste was able to say she had Autism too.

At the time of this event I had a lovely lady by the name of Skye visiting two days a week to care for Celeste. This gave me two days of uninterrupted time so I could focus on work and writing. It also meant that I could sneak out from time to time to attend appointments or just have time for myself. Skye was amazing. She was a mother herself and although she had very little understanding of Autism when she first started working for me she soon worked Celeste out, being able to keep her calm and engage her in undertaking tasks that enhanced her skills. Celeste quickly fell in love with Skye, looking forward to the two days of the week where she was the centre of attention, engaging in fun games and lots of craft. On occasions Skye would bring her children with her, thereby adding to Celeste's socialisation experiences. The four children got on well, enjoying each other's company. Skye was with us for about a year but unfortunately, due to us moving from the area and Skye seeking full time employment, we parted ways. Still today Celeste misses her friend.

Another book event that saw us socialising with Minnie was that of the children's picture book 'Ben and Buddy' by Kerrie Uren. This book is based around Buddy, Kerrie's own Greyhound, who finds his forever home after being put up for adoption with Greyhounds New Beginnings. It is a sweet story that speaks of the bond between a Greyhound and his foster child, Ben, who later gets to keep Buddy. It speaks of the adjustments Greyhounds must make when going from track to house and the beautiful nature of Greys. It is a gentle and touching introduction for children into

Greyhounds, adoption and the bonding of a dog. 'Ben and Buddy' is a regular read in our house with Celeste loving the story of another Grey. She can often be found sitting on the floor looking at the pictures with Minnie, telling Minnie all about the story.

We were lucky enough to be invited to be part of the release of 'Ben and Buddy', which was held at Mad Hatters Bookstore in Manly, Queensland. This was a lovely little event which included a few other Greys. Minnie and Celeste were placed in the thick of it as I was asked to support Buffy from Greyhounds New Beginnings as she gave a speech about what they do. Buffy introduced us and I spoke of Minnie's role in our life. Both Minnie and Celeste did me proud, standing by my side, Minnie ready to help Celeste if she needed her. The bookshop was only small so soon became crowded. Celeste held herself together holding Minnie for support, using her to keep a space between herself and all the people.

When in shopping centres one of Minnie's major roles is that of guiding Celeste as she walks along, keeping herself between Celeste and people. Being touched by others, be it even the slightest of knocks as someone walks past, will cause Celeste to meltdown. When walking, Celeste has no spacial awareness, running into people and objects and walking a zigzag path. Holding onto Minnie's coat as she walks, with Minnie touching her leg, gives her direction. Minnie will stop if Celeste balks or falls behind and directs Celeste around people and items. With a verbal direction of 'this way' Minnie will direct Celeste in the direction I have gestured. People notice Minnie which means they notice Celeste, leading them to be less likely to brush against her. They tend to take a wider berth when they see an assistance dog, giving the person extra consideration and space.

Another role we have taken on since Minnie came along is that of supporting Smart Pups Assistance Dogs. It is the least we can do as a thank you for all the support they give us. The charity is close to our hearts. Having experienced first hand what Minnie has done for my child I know all too well the benefits of a Smart Pup. If we can help achieve a dog for just one child then we will have contributed to changing a life. If, via Smart Pups, we can raise awareness of the loving calm nature of Greyhounds and their ability to be certified assistance dogs, then changing the life of at least one Grey is an achievement. I acknowledge that Greyhounds are not suitable for all children with Autism due to the fact that they are more delicate in frame than Labradors and Retrievers and autistic children can be violent and are strong, but I am confident that with time we will see this breed being used with children more often. Celeste speaks of her hope that more children will have a Greyhound to love. In her eyes all children need a friend like Minnie.

One event for Smart Pups that sticks in my mind is that of the barefoot bowling fundraiser we attended. We were meant to attend as part of the Smart Pups team, amongst trainers and other dogs, but on the day severe storms hit meaning Smart Pups was unable to drive all the way from the Sunshine Coast to Brisbane. I was not aware of this though until I arrived at the event to find that Minnie, Celeste and I were it. Would I mind giving a little talk on behalf of Smart Pups? Although I was familiar with speaking in front of people I was hesitant as I had not been with Smart Pups for long and was unsure of what to say. My speech was to follow that of a gentleman who spoke about beyondblue, a not for profit organisation who educate and support Australians in regards to mental health issues, so I listened attentively to what he had to say, hoping I could bounce off the information he provided. This gentleman's speech blew me away as he spoke of depression and suicide, two things that have been part of Alex's life. He spoke of the need for support and awareness and of the work beyondblue did. As I listened and related to his words, what I was going to talk about hit me. I cannot clearly remember what I actually said but I referred to his speech adding my own honest experiences. I spoke of the anxiety Celeste feels each day and of the depression that often goes hand in hand with Alex's Autism. I spoke of how Minnie assists Celeste on a daily basis, helping her stay calm when the anxiety gets too much and providing an outlet for a calming pat and listening ear when Celeste is not coping. I spoke of the gentle training of Smart Pups and how these dogs, regardless of breed are changing the lives of families. I felt empowered by the questions people asked and the connection I had with them after my speech when we hung around for a while so people could meet Minnie and Celeste. At the end of the day the gentleman from beyondblue thanked me for my wonderful talk and for following up on what he had said, incorporating it with information about Smart Pups. I never found out if the event raised any funds for Smart Pups but was given positive feedback and thanks for attending. For myself it is not about the thanks but about the touching of hearts, changing of lives and educating of others. The socialisation that Celeste undertakes, the being placed in a situation she has never been in before, learning coping skills and the building of her self esteem as she is recognised and her dog praised, is what she takes away from it all. Minnie laps up the attention. At these events I place her in a down and allow people to pat her and talk to her, allowing her to spread some love and receive love in return.

Christmas is a hard time for children but for a child with Autism it is one of confusion and sensory overload. The anticipation of Santa quickly becomes too much. The changes in the shops, the Christmas music and the extra people soon cause overload. There are lights which flash colour and society's expectations for us to attend events add pressure. Even the TV viewing changes. For a little over a month the world is full of change, change, change. By the time Christmas Day arrives Celeste is in full meltdown mode and I am tearing my hair out.

One thing every parent wants, and I am not excluded, is a decent photo of their child on Santa's knee. I do question why. I suppose it is one of those things you are expected to do as a parent, left to feel you are letting your child down if you do not have one Santa photo for them to look back at when they get older.

Minnie's first Christmas with us was one of excitement. Usually Celeste would stand a mile from Santa and wave to him. There would be meltdown after meltdown as each time we visited the shops she geared herself up to go and say hello to Santa but failed when the time came. She felt like a failure, unable to meet her own goals. This first year, with Minnie, was the year. For the first time the local shopping centre was taking part in Sensory Santa. This is a special Santa who is aware of Autism and special needs. During the allocated time the lights are dimmed, music turned down and Santa is open only for booked visits. Santa has no expectations of the children sitting on his knee and does not offer a handshake or cuddle unless this is initiated by the child. A friendly smile and interest in the child is the only thing offered. Time is taken to allow the child to get to know him. Seats, reindeers, soft toys and all things non threatening are provided around Santa allowing the children to get as close to, or stay as far away from him as they are comfortable with for a photo. This year was the year I was to get my first decent photo of Celeste with Santa, a photo I am proud of years, and many Santa photos later. For the first time Celeste stood beside Santa and smiled. With Minnie leaning against the front of her legs she was invincible. With confidence she told Santa what she wanted for Christmas and spoke to him about Minnie. Santa promised to leave Minnie a special treat as she was a very special dog.

Many doors have opened over the years of having Minnie in our lives with opportunities that have been both planned and spontaneous. All of these have been positive steps forward. All of them have been thanks to Minnie.

# A RARE HOLIDAY...

With Minnie came the ability to have a holiday. Our first break from home in a very long time and our first holiday with Minnie would incorporate work and fun. Our friend Dawn and her Greyhound assistance dog, Lucy, were holding a gallery display titled 'Sonata in Z' at the Nick Waterlow Gallery, UNSW Art and Design, Paddington, Sydney, as part of Dawn's studies. This display was based around sensory experiences and Autism and Dawn had invited us to attend. Evan Shapiro, author of the book 'A Road to Nowhere', who was initially a business friend of mine but had become a work colleague and friend, also resided in Sydney. Having worked with Evan online, not only supporting his writing but introducing clients to his graphic design and publishing business, I felt it was time that we met face to face. With Minnie showing strength in her ability to help Celeste I felt it was as good a time as ever to brave a trip to Sydney. The trip one way by car from Ipswich to Sydney was approximately 10 hours. My mother resides in Nabiac NSW which was basically the halfway point, so it was arranged that I would travel to Mum's, where I would stay the night and leave Beauty to be babysat, and then travel from Nabiac to Sydney where I would stay in a motel. This would lessen the hours Celeste was in the car in one day and allow her to visit her Nanna. This would be Minnie's second trip to Nanna's as we had taken her to meet Nanna prior to her training.

My mother had two small poodles whom we initially had concerns for around Minnie. One was a toy poodle with the other being a miniature. It was the toy poodle that worried me the most as he sat no bigger than a cat, if not smaller. At the time of our initial visit to my mum's we had no idea how Minnie would behave around small dogs. She was getting used to the cats but a little fluffy dog was a different story. On first introduction I held Minnie on-lead ready to recall her quickly if she should attack. I need not have worried. She sniffed and wagged her tail. She then proceeded to turn away, showing no further interest. Placing her muzzle on, as we had done for our cats, I took her off-lead. She went in the opposite direction. The first time Ebon walked by I held my breath, actually I think he walked right between her legs under her tummy and out the other side without a need to duck. Minnie took no notice. We were soon able to confidently remove the muzzle and poodles and Greyhound became best friends.

I remember the day Minnie decided that if the dog bed was good enough for a poodle it was good enough for her. Here was a long legged Greyhound doing twirlies to get comfortable around a bed that was not much bigger than her head circumference. I watched with laughter asking her if she seriously thought she was going to fit. They say that if it is comfy and soft it is made for a Grey, and how true this is. Here was Minnie curled in a ball on a pink bed that disappeared under her. Her bum fitted and that was all that mattered. She hung her head over the edge looking proud. This soon became her 'comfy' place each time she visited.

Our trip to Sydney would be a quick one. In total we would be gone 4 days. Expense had to be considered, along with time away from the cats. A friend had kindly offered to feed the cats for us so Alex could come with us. Although quick, I felt it would test Celeste's ability to cope, challenge my ability to handle an assistance dog in different situations and allow me a much needed break from staring at the walls of my home.

Taking children on holidays, regardless of how long or where, takes consideration and planning. Taking an anxious child with an assistance dog can double the planning. After searching online for a motel I chose a budget chain of motels that was close to Evan's house and within driving distance to the university. Before booking online I rang them to let them know I would be bringing an assistance dog with me. I had read on the Smart Pups Facebook page of others who were having problems with motels so I was expecting a battle. To my surprise the lovely lady said it was fine. Just to be on the safe side I added a message when booking online, receiving a reply that stated they welcomed Minnie and they would see us on the day. All easier than I thought.

The day before departing we packed the car. In order to lessen the anxiety and to keep Celeste focussed, I engaged her in packing the items we would need for Minnie: food bowl, water bowl, a refillable bottle for water, food, treats, poop bags, lead, her assistance dog coat, a coat as it was cool, and her bed. Silly Mummy nearly forgot Minnie's favourite squeaky toy.

With excitement running through her blood, and toys on her mind, Celeste then proceeded to pack her own toys. I had to remind her that we only have an 8 seater people mover not a truck. The meltdown began. The decision of what toys to take and the realisation she would be away from her things for a few days dawned on her. All activity was aborted as Minnie sat with her, calming her. She soon announced that Minnie had it all worked out and that her toys would keep each other company until she returned. As long as she took Woody, Buzz and a few of her special friends the rest would be waiting for her return. She is a clever girl, our Minnie. She always knows what to say at the right time, not like Mum who would only be putting silly words into Celeste's head and suggesting things that made no sense. Life with Celeste is about empowering her so that she feels in control of the decision making and the situation as a whole.

With a 6 hour drive to my mother's we started our trip at the early hour of 6:00am. The customary McDonald's detour for a drive thru breakfast was in order. Same as usual, hash browns, English muffin with jam, the biggest cappuccino they have for Mummy and a hot chocolate with marshmallows for Celeste and Alex. The hot chocolate was thrown in due to the cold weather but Celeste still had to have her apple juice as one cannot divert from routine. We can add something but we are never, never, never to take anything away. As we travelled Alex sat in the front seat with Minnie sitting on the car seat beside Celeste. Beauty travelled on the floor between the two front seats. I glanced in the rear view mirror to see Minnie with her nose resting on Celeste's lap. I am sure the smell of the food must have been making her hungry but I never need to worry about her stealing food from Celeste as she is trained to 'leave it' and discipline is something she takes seriously.

I can usually get about an hour's travel out of Celeste before trouble hits and this trip was no exception. At about the hour mark the iPad had lost its appeal, the toys were all over the floor of the car and the food had gone cold. The incessant speech and fidgeting had started. This would soon lead to screaming, crying, kicking the car seat and verbal abuse that no amount of coercing would calm her. Thankfully our first routine rest area was near. It was important that if we were going to do the same long trip regularly, we put a routine into place and stuck to it. This gives Celeste some understanding of the events that are happening. This routine needs to be given great thought, down to every little detail. I need to make sure I can live up to what Celeste expects each and every time. Sometimes things happen that are out of my control, such as a café or service station closes, meaning that for the next few trips hell lets loose until Celeste is comfortable with the changes. Walking out the door and enjoying themselves is something most families take for granted, but that can't be done with Autism.

Many years ago, as we were driving by an independent fruit stall on the side of the road, evident by the large banana sitting on the top of it, Sam noticed the price of the bananas which was quite high and made a statement along the lines of wondering if anyone stops and buys them. Now, years later, every time we drive past the store, Celeste mimics Sam word for word. It always makes me smile but the problem is that she expects me to answer her with the exact answer I gave Sam. This now causes anxiety as, unlike her, I cannot remember what I said and she cannot understand why. Echolalia, the repetition of vocalisations made by another person, is a common characteristic of Autism. This may be immediate, as when the person repeats the phrase or sound immediately, or may be delayed anywhere from hours to years. Echolalia is a way of making sense of language and the world around you. Celeste's echolalia is different from her need to repeat actions and routines on a daily basis. The echolalia events occur when she finds herself in the same situation or revisits a particular place. These can be months or years apart and cause much distress to all as she melts down due to my lack of awareness or memory that we even did something a particular way on the previous occasion. I can clearly remember this happening with Alex, although not as severely, when he was young, but now, as a young adult, he has found other ways to make sense of life. I hope, with time and the help of Minnie, Celeste will put into place skills that helps her 'normalise' her understanding of the world around her.

With our regular rest stops we made it my mum's just after lunch. As Alex and I piled out of the car Celeste became anxious about the need to take all her toys into Nanna's. As I walked around to her side of the car and slid open the side door she stood while trying to pile her arms with her many toys. Nanna had come out to say hello and the pressure Celeste felt to be out of the car and seeing Nanna escalated. For Celeste, being first, which I suppose is a form of control for her own comfort and the inability to see outside of her own needs, was important. If you approach someone before her she will barge past you. You are not to walk down a hallway or through a door before Celeste, nor in front of her. If Celeste is behind, another episode of abuse and headbanging will follow. Consideration, politeness and the fact that you do not need to be first is something we work hard at with Celeste. Minnie gives us a hand here, standing beside Celeste, teaching her about togetherness and thinking about others. With Minnie being the focus of others when we are out with her, Celeste has, over time, learnt that it is okay for another to be noticed. Minnie is teaching her the basic rules of socialisation.

As Nanna got closer to the car the meltdown escalated. Here I was trying to cope with two dogs who were eager to get out of the car and a child who was headbanging and screaming. By now Alex had got out of the car and said hello to Nanna, only making the meltdown worse as Celeste screamed that she wanted to say hello first. It always surprises me how others seem to be oblivious to what is happening, with my mum focussed only on the fact that we had arrived. As Nanna approached the car and focussed her attention on Celeste the meltdown began to subside. Nanna asked Celeste what was wrong and when told she couldn't carry all her toys Nanna offered to help her. It is times like these that my blood boils. I want to scream. Here I was, only seconds beforehand, calmly talking to Celeste over her screaming, telling her that I would help her, trying to encourage her to get out of the car with just a few toys in her hand and I would get the rest. Here I was, only moments ago, being called an idiot, hit and told I just did not understand. One word from Nanna and life is okay. It is hard to explain these situations. It is often suggested to me by people who have only just met Celeste that these meltdowns are simply a child being naughty and wanting her own way. There is a huge difference between an autistic meltdown and a spoilt brat meltdown. The way in which it happens, the body language, the confusion on the face, the inability to process what is being said and the inability to make sense of the surroundings are only an example of the extent of a meltdown due to Autism. It is not until one has seen Celeste experience one of these episodes on a few occasions that one sees it for what it is.

The evening went well with time spent sitting around the house enjoying the company of family. Minnie remembered her poodle friends, settling into her little pink poodle bed for the night. As bedtime neared the normal attempt to get Celeste into a bath or shower in a strange house began. Minnie was called upon to accompany Celeste and encourage her to bathe. On this occasion, like many others when we visited Nanna, it was not to happen. Still today I have been unable to understand why there is a fear of bathing in a different bathroom, but again this was a problem experienced with Alex as well. Bathtime has always been a nightmare in our house. Thankfully by the time Celeste was out of the baby years and the really big struggles had begun Alex had put strategies into play that enable him to cope.

For me bathtime with Celeste is like running a marathon. I leave the bathroom physically and mentally exhausted from the battle. The bath must be filled without Celeste in the bathroom as the noise of the running water causes her to cover her ears and rock. It is loud and scares her, although she knows what it is and what it is doing. Once the bath is filled, or the shower turned on, there is the battle to undress her as she struggles with the clothing and the changes in feeling against the skin. Celeste must put her hand in the water and then, regardless of temperature, it is always a little bit hot and she must see me run the cold water for a second. I must not turn the cold water off until she yells stop and then my turning it off must be instant or it is followed with repetitive screaming and abuse. It is all in the timing. Bathtime is another example of obsession over detail of routine. Hair is only washed when really dirty and necessary, eliminating one part of the sensory overload battle. You don't even want to start me on the brushing of the hair and tying it up after a bath or each morning. On many occasions Celeste has left the house with matted, unkempt hair as I battle the voice in my head that say I can't take her out like that with the one that says does it really matter, leave it so we have one less battle getting out the door.

The bath and the hair seem to be two things that Minnie cannot bring calm to. Due to the size of the bathroom and the behaviour of Celeste I no longer involve Minnie in the bath battle as her safety needs to be considered. When brushing the hair we sit at the dining room table where Minnie places her head on Celeste's lap. Celeste strokes her and watches YouTube on her iPad as a diversion, but still we meltdown. As time has passed the hair brushing meltdown has lessened in intensity as Celeste tells Minnie and me all about what is on the iPad. For myself this is a mentally exhausting job as I hastily brush and tie while battling to keep the attention on anything but the brush.

Sleeping at Nanna's was thankfully a breeze as we were able to follow the same routine of Celeste sleeping in a double bed with me, making sure I went to bed at the same time as her. Nanna had a pile of picture books ready for the grandkids and Celeste loved to sit on her lap and listen to a book before bed. Minnie was quite happy to curl up on the double bed close to her girl.

An early rise and a three hour trip, with breaks of course, saw us arrive safe and sound in Sydney. On this occasion Celeste coped well with Minnie by her side even though she had not been to Sydney before. Being born in Sydney and spending the first 32 years of my life there I was able to fill her head with stories of my childhood, pointing out landmarks, building it all into a calm adventure. There was one occasion where the going got a bit tough when we were stuck in traffic and I was lost, not being able to find the motel. The panic of being lost and being stuck in the car became real for Celeste, but with encouragement to help Mummy focus on what the GPS was saying, we soon got out of our pickle.

We arrived at the motel and piled out of the car with relief that we had made it. Even though I had been told Minnie was welcome, I approached the office with trepidation. Experience had taught me that what is said in email is not always the situation when you arrive. As I entered the reception area, with children and dog in tow, I was welcomed with the smiling face of a lovely lady who did not bat an eyelid at the sight of Minnie. The welcoming hospitality continued as we were checked in and given the key to our room. It was then that I looked around me and realised that all I could see for kilometres was a concrete jungle. The motel was situated on a main street surrounded by shops.

This was great for grabbing a bite or two to eat but not great for an assistance dog who needs grass to toilet. I also realised it had been a while since Minnie had gone to the toilet.

With key in hand we set off down the street to see if we could find somewhere to toilet Minnie. Coming to a corner about 250 metres down the road I was relieved to see a small car park used for the block of shops next to the motel. The grass was a sparse strip but it was grass, dirty with litter but still grass. Giving Minnie the 'quick quick' command for toilet I walked the small patch waiting patiently for her to toilet. She sniffed the ground, only briefly, and then, holding her head high looked at me as if to say, "You are kidding right?" With it obvious she was not going to go we decided to find our room and come back for a 'quick, quick' shortly.

Our motel room was on the third floor, a lift being our mode of entry and exit. The door of the room faced onto a cement quadrangle with a verandah facing the back of the motel, overlooking more concrete quadrangles. I was finding myself facing new challenges with an assistance dog and child. We would need to find a park to run or go for a very long walk around the block.

I had arranged to have coffee with Evan at his house that afternoon so it was back in the car for Celeste, Minnie and me. Alex, not feeling comfortable with socialising and being a teenager who needed some technology time, had decided to stay behind in the motel, with, of course, stern instructions from myself not to open the door. The drive to Evan's was only fifteen minutes so we soon arrived at our destination and were enjoying coffee and cake with a friend. With Evan having a multi media room, Celeste enjoyed her visit, settling with a movie. Minnie was not too sure about staying in the multi media room, wanting to leave Celeste, even though I told her to stay, and return to me. Being a three part team, she seemed a little confused at to what her role was when I was not by Celeste's side. She was torn between who she should be with. I continued to return her to Celeste, giving her commands, until she settled. More learning for all involved.

Next call was takeaway from the Indian restaurant below the motel. Minnie still had not toileted so back to our little grass patch we went while we waited for our food. Still no 'quick, quick'. Minnie didn't seem worried but I was stressed. What if she got an infection from not peeing? How can she not need to pee; it has been hours and many drinks of water later?

With our bellies full and after resting watching TV, the sun began to set. Minnie had also eaten and had a drink. She had enjoyed curling up with Celeste as they watched their favourite shows. As dark set in I decided that it was time for one last attempt at 'quick, quick' before retiring for the night. Celeste and I set out in the dark for a walk, hoping that if we walked the block Minnie would find a pleasant smell that she just had to pee on. Being in the city meant there was plenty of light and activity for us to feel safe. Our walk was unproductive. No 'quick quick'. Celeste was now becoming anxious about what would happen to Minnie if she did not pee or poo. What would happen if she needed to go in the middle of the night? Minnie nuzzled Celeste reassuring her that she was fine. I am sure she understands every word we say. This was enough reassurance for Celeste to tell me that Minnie would work it out. She would let us know when she needed to toilet. Words are never needed between these two.

A quick sponge down for Celeste and teeth brushed and we retired together in the big double bed. Being away for only one night, and with there being no bath in the motel, I was not going to stress her about showering. I was an expert at sponge bathing her from top to toe, getting her sparkling clean and relaxed. Minnie curled up next to Celeste looking exhausted after her long day. I had told myself that if she did have an accident overnight the room was tiled and I would easily be able to clean up her mess. I need not have worried as she slept soundly.

As soon as I woke the next morning I threw some clothes on, and leaving Celeste in the care of Alex for a few minutes, I took Minnie downstairs to the grass. Still no 'quick, quick.' That was it. I was fed up with the worry. She would go when she needed to and there was nothing I could do about it. Coffee and breakfast and then time to start our day. We had an exhibit to attend.

Our drive to the university where Dawn's exhibit was being held was eventful. The deeper into the city we got the more stressed Celeste became. The excitement of where we were going caused the anxiety. By the time we arrived at the event Celeste had a headache and was wanting to throw up.

The exhibit was amazing! It brought Celeste peace. For everyone it was a tranquil sensory experience. The calming music, the relaxing white colour, the soft texture of materials and the silent welcoming were a blessing. Celeste spent time doing relaxing craft and found the soft, smooth, slimy orby balls heaven. It was just what was needed after a few hectic days.

Minnie had a wonderful time also. She met Lucy, Dawn's Greyhound assistance dog, and enjoyed the treats Dawn had prepared. She still had not done her 'quick, quick' and it was here she disgraced me for the first time. Obviously not being able to hold on any longer she decided that a soft rug Dawn had placed on the ground was a good place to squat. As soon as I saw her squatting I knew what she was about to do, quickly yelling 'no' whilst instructing Alex to watch Celeste for me. I grabbed Minnie's lead and ran with her as fast as I could out the exit. Taking her outside I found the only bit of grass amongst this once again concrete jungle. I stood telling her 'quick, quick' but she would not go. What! I was fuming. It took all my compassion for her and the situation nor to yell at her. I was beginning to feel that being on a lead and not peeing had reared its ugly head again because I realised that when inside she was not on-lead. I walked back inside feeling deflated. Dawn soon came to my rescue suggesting we take both dogs outside for a walk, maybe Minnie would toilet if Lucy did. We walked them both down the pathway toward a garden area, where Lucy did her pee. At first I felt our plan was a failure but as we watched, waited and encouraged Minnie she watched Lucy, sniffed where she had peed and squatted. YAY! We had success. After twenty four hours,Minnie had done a pee.

After bidding Dawn and Lucy a farewell, and with a huge teddy and stuffed dog that took the whole back seat of my car as a gift, we started our three hour drive back to Nabiac where we would once again stay overnight, collecting Beauty and travelling the rest of the trip home the next morning. I was glad to leave the concrete jungle and I am sure Minnie was too. The toileting issue was over as we found grass or dirt in rest areas on the way home. This would not be the last time Minnie would disgrace herself in regards to toileting.

About a year later, I was placed in a most embarrassing situation in regards to Minnie's bowel motions. This happened at our local shopping centre, causing it to be weeks after the event before I could face going back due to my own embarrassment. Minnie was most upset and apologetic. Unbeknown to me, she had a belly ache. It was mid morning and as far as I knew she had been fine at home all morning, although I will admit I do not follow her around outside and watch her bowel movements.

We drove to the local shopping centre, parked, suggested toilet to Minnie as we usually do before entering the centre and when she did not go continued with walking into the shopping centre. As I walked through the doors Minnie slowed and pulled back on her lead a little. I noticed it but just spoke gently to her telling her to come. A few minutes later she was doubling her body over and looking at me sorrowfully as diarrhea came out her rear end. I was beside myself not knowing what to do. I was telling Minnie 'no' but I knew she was in trouble with pain and that she was not doing it on purpose. The only thing I could think of was to get her out of the centre but how. As I took a step forward she stayed doubled over, the diarrhoea continuing. By this stage everyone in the shopping centre was looking at me and Celeste was panicking. Not one person offered me assistance. As I started rummaging through my bag looking for my poop bags, thinking that maybe if I held one over her bottom I could at least catch the poop until I thought of how I was going to get her out, a gentleman from centre management came over.

I never got to thank this man but to me he was a saviour. He got on his two way radio and called for a cleaner. All I could do was stand there and apologise, letting him know that she was trained and obviously wasn't well. Had I known I would not have brought her out. He spoke gently to me, said it was okay and he could see that she had a belly ache. As Minnie stood normally again and the diarrhoea had stopped, I suggested to him that I get her out of the centre and take her home. Naturally he agreed but it meant that I left him and the cleaner with the mess. The cleaner was not as nice as the gentleman, actually being quite rude. She grunted her disapproval and gave me the filthiest of looks as she put gloves on. I just smiled at her but what I really want to do was yell at her and ask her if she thought I had got the dog to do it on purpose. I wanted to remind her that she did get paid to clean.

When we did eventually return to the centre all was okay. Minnie is still welcome and the situation forgotten. Centre management handled the whole thing with professionalism, making me and Celeste feel welcome back. As for the cleaner, at least she had something to complain about that afternoon. Minnie has never disgraced me since and was sorry for days afterwards. She was terribly embarrassed.

# NEW AREA, NEW CHALLENGES

As the relationship between Minnie and Celeste grew so did our family, both furry and human. Being a single mum of special needs children was not only a challenge but often a lonely time. With family so far away the only contact I had with anyone on most days was with my children. It was hard to meet others when your life revolved around making sure the emotional and mental health of your child was at its optimum at all times. It was also a big expectation to ask any man to accept us into his life as his family and understand the struggles of our day to day living, but it happened. I met a wonderful man and life changes began.

Introducing Shane to Celeste went more smoothly than I anticipated. I had naturally discussed my life with him so he was well prepared. He was the father of an adult daughter so the fact that he had experience with children gave me hope. We had decided that the best way to introduce him into the lives of both Celeste and Alex was to do so in the secure environment of their own home. They would not feel threatened by sensory changes, being able to ignore Shane and go about their day as usual. Another bonus in the whole introduction was that Shane loved dogs, having a fur baby of his own who he dotted on. We discussed introducing Shane's dog Roxy to Celeste and Minnie in the first instance as we felt this would be a great ice breaker but Roxy was not great around cats so we felt it better to leave the cat issue to another time as this may cause extra stress on all involved. Shane would tell Celeste about Roxy when asking her about Minnie, creating common ground. The first meeting between Shane and Celeste went well, which was actually the first face to face meeting between Shane and myself. Having talked to Shane for some time online we felt we knew each other quite well, causing our face to face meeting to only strengthen our connection. Minnie loved the attention Shane gave her. She soaked up every pat as Shane used his magic to win over both her and Celeste.

New Year's Eve was upon us a few days after our first introduction. This was a great time to take Celeste out and give Shane a chance to experience my life out and about. The year prior I had attended a family event at the local oval which Celeste had enjoyed. It was a free event which was kid orientated with rides, shows and lots of food. We would stay for the 9pm fireworks, returning home afterwards to see in the new year with Alex. This would be the first year I had taken Minnie to the event.

With fold-out chairs organised we looked forward to a wonderful night of all getting to know each other. With the event being in a large open space there would be plenty of room for Celeste to run and room for her to sit with Minnie. We found a nice area not far from the stage and got ourselves comfy for the night. Leaving our chairs to save our spot we spent some time, upon request of Celeste, lining up, waiting for rides. With the comfort of Minnie, we made it to the end of some lines. In other queues, we waited for so long that Celeste's anxiety eventually become overbearing so we left. The decision to leave, which had to be Celeste's, only came after a lengthy time of incessant repetitive talk, rocking, headbanging and throwing herself on the ground. Minnie was working hard laying herself across Celeste while she lay on the ground, calming her. Each time Minnie leant on Celeste she would talk to her and Minnie would look Celeste in the eyes, using body language and her connection to tell Celeste she could do this. The meltdowns were not over once Celeste decided she didn't want to wait as she then felt she had failed herself, headbanging and often running back to the line confused about whether she should leave or not. Each time she ran Minnie would stand strong and turn toward Celeste not allowing me to take another step unless that step was to take her back to get her girl and calm her. It took time and a lot of patience on my part but eventually we were able to get food and agree that settling in our chairs to watch the shows was where we needed to be. Shane's introduction to time out with Celeste was surely a trying one.

He stood beside me supporting me while allowing me to handle the situation. He offered to hold Minnie's lead when he felt it would help and interacted with Celeste in a calm manner.

What we had not thought through was the fireworks. I had experienced these with Celeste in previous years and although she covered her ears and hid under a blanket snuggling me she loved to watch them. What we neglected to think about was the reaction of dogs to fireworks. I suppose the thought didn't cross my mind as by this stage I was just used to taking Minnie everywhere with us, appreciating the help she gave me with Celeste. It was hard to imagine life without her. Minnie had been tested against sudden noises and bangs and coped marvellously but these, of course, were not the extreme bang of fireworks. As soon as the fireworks started I knew we were in trouble. It was the longest fireworks' display I have ever had to sit through. Thank God for the help of Shane. Minnie panicked. Her flight instinct set in as she pulled back on her lead. My instant reaction was to get down on the ground next to her and wrap my arms around her. Our poor girl was shaking. With Shane holding her lead and cuddling her from behind, I sat beside her head, leaning my head on hers, speaking calming words to her. As I did so I scanned our surroundings trying to find a way to get her out but we were hemmed in by the crowd. It also occurred to me that we would have to carry her out as she would not walk due to panic. The only thing I could do was sit with her. Celeste soon realised what was happening, taking the chance to comfort her girl. She took the other side of Minnie's front and cuddled in, also speaking to her softly about how pretty the fireworks looked. I am sure we were a strange sight. Three humans and one dog huddled together as if it was the end of the world. While all this was going on a positive had come out of it. Celeste had shown compassion, love and comfort to another, removing herself from her own world to place herself into understanding how Minnie was feeling. Here was a little girl who would normally be so focussed on coping with her own anxiety over the fireworks doing something she had not done before. Through Minnie she had shown empathy.

As soon as the fireworks finished Minnie was back to normal. As the crowd dispersed we sat with her a while as I did not feel it was fair that she be made to work hard at helping Celeste manoeuvre her way through the crowd after feeling traumatised herself. When all had settled I took my position on her right, Celeste held her coat on the left and Shane grabbed the chairs. We headed home with Shane and I discussing how we never wanted to go through that again. To my surprise Shane kept visiting.

As our family relationship grew so did the challenges. Alex took a while to warm up to Shane with a few hiccups along the way needing time and gentleness to help sort them out. As Celeste became more comfortable with Shane he too became an 'idiot' and she hated him: words she threw at people when experiencing a meltdown. He too became the victim of having things thrown at him and of experiencing Celeste's headbanging response. The pressure on our relationship was immense but we kept on going, to the extent that the kids and I were soon packing up house and moving from Ipswich to the Gold Coast. The changes had become huge.

Prior to moving we were spending half our week at Shane's and half at my house. The dogs were getting along nicely and Roxy was leaving the cats alone, although we were cautious and kept an eye on her. Minnie was working extremely hard. Although we tried to keep the changes for Celeste to a minimum things just changed naturally without us realising. With Shane coming into my life, Celeste sharing a bed with me was no longer appropriate. Prior to Minnie coming into our lives, I had tried many times to relocate Celeste to a bed of her own. I knew a room of her own was too big a step so had tried mattresses on the floor in my room. This had never worked as she needed body contact and pressure to sleep. Minnie came to the rescue. Having Minnie lie on the bed against Celeste at night and Celeste being able to cuddle her friend gave her the security she needed to make a move out of Mum's bed. We still did it in stages. For months she slept on a mattress on the floor next to my side of the bed. Here she had the comfort of Mum, with myself having to start the night with my hand hanging over the edge of the bed while I held her hand. With a night light and pressure from Minnie we slowly got a night's sleep. I was soon able to remove my contact with Minnie taking over completely.

The moving to her own bedroom took some time. We tried a few times at Ipswich but the anxiety was so high that, even with Minnie by her side, she could not last long. We tried music so that it was not too quiet and she sang to Minnie but still she felt anxious. I would lie in my bed on the other side of the hallway on these nights and listen to her one sided conversation with Minnie. A sweet little voice would float across the hall, ever so gentle as she told Minnie that it was okay, she could do this. If Minnie was okay with it she was too, after all Mummy was close by. In between these conversations she would scream at me telling me she couldn't do it. I would hear her bang the walls and hear the thump of her wrist as it hit her head. Moments like these hurt me as all I could do was respond with reassurance. I had learnt in the early days that adding my words or suggestions just added confusion to her mind. On these nights as we prepared for bed I would watch as she settled Minnie on the bed, making sure she was covered with a blanket and close enough for cuddles. She would gently speak to Minnie asking her if she was warm enough and reassuring her that she need not be scared as she was there for her. Through Minnie she lived her own fears, facing them head on. Facing fears with a friend is always so much easier than doing it alone.

When we moved to the Gold Coast Celeste was still in the main bedroom on a mattress on the floor but soon gained enough confidence to move herself and Minnie into a room near ours. This started with Shane creating her a beautiful room full of shelves, her bed and toys. As a family unit we spent time creating a comfortable place for her and Minnie. We allowed Celeste to feel in control while we guided her. She would spend the days in the room, first with me and Minnie, then with Minnie alone, just playing and exploring. She would take Minnie for a 'tour' around the room, pointing out where her toys and clothes were kept and walking her through what was on her pretty pink shelves. One day while I was observing them it occurred to me that Minnie was smiling. Her whole face was glowing as her girl devoted her time to her. The love between the two of them was mutual. Their friendship was benefiting Minnie as well as Celeste.

These days Minnie is no longer required at night, but she is still there. She stays a while until she is sure Celeste is asleep and then she sneaks out, just like a mum would, to have her alone time on the lounge. Our cat, Millie, has taken over the night time duty. She took it upon herself when we moved to make Celeste hers, curling up on the bed each night and living her days in Celeste's room. Our other cat, Jimbo, chose Alex years ago and has become a great therapy cat for Alex, who has always needed a cat as therapy. For Alex the soft feel of a cat and the gentle purr is his comfort. Jimbo can be seen every morning curled up under Alex chin with the blankets over him. Both children share the feeding of the cats, Celeste being in charge of nighttime tin food, both being responsible for water and dry food for their own cat. The healing power of animals of all descriptions has been proven in this house.

Moving house is not easy for anyone. For Celeste, grasping the whole concept and placing her belongings into boxes was something that had to be done over a period of time. The living between two house for a few months helped dramatically by allowing her to assimilate to her new environment, but the one and a half hour travel from one house to another was never easy. I tried to encourage her to have some toys at Shane's and some at ours but this caused more anxiety than it was worth. Then there was the anxiety about what to take from one house to another each time. During this period her rat, Rufus, was still with us. Rufus was Celeste's baby. Minnie was her forever friend but Rufus was her baby. Each day she cuddled him, dressed him up and nurtured him. Rufus had a carry bag so he could sit beside Celeste in the car but there was his large cage to be transported from one house to another and all his belongings.

Anxiety was created each time as Celeste panicked that she had forgotten something. We discussed buying Rufus another cage but Celeste was clear that he loved his house and there would be no other.

During this period Minnie was worth more than gold. She was Celeste's rock. She comforted her on our drives and was by her side to explore her new environment. Importance was placed on taking Minnie for walks and to the dog parks and on creating a comfortable environment in our new home for Minnie. Placing the attention on Minnie and using Minnie as our model we were able to introduce new experiences and situations. Setting up scenarios with Minnie as the star of the situation created a non threatening situation where Celeste was able to stay calm while making sense of what was happening and relate Minnie's feelings to her own.

During this transition period, I packed a box or two each day we were at the house in Ipswich. In the beginning, when there were only a few boxes, these were left in the study out of sight but as the number of boxes grew, and I needed more storage room, they were progressed to the lounge room.

It was then that plan B was put into place, involving Celeste by giving her tasks. Having Celeste engage in the packing by writing (copying) the contents onto the box with marker or drawing pictures was a small thing that was two-fold in purpose as it also engaged her in words and writing. She was put in charge of the packing tape or given water to clean cupboards. Packing at night after she had gone to sleep was another way I did it but she always reacted to the change. I was amazed that even if I had only packed or moved one box she knew the next morning. During all of this it was important that the TV was not moved or disconnected and neither was the internet. The familiarity of her TV programs and YouTube were the two things she could have that made sense. With a blanket on the floor or curled up on the lounge she would lie with Minnie for hours on end, immersed in her visual world, stroking Minnie and forgetting about the changes around her. Minnie loves TV, being a dedicated watcher of ABC Kids, but she always found it hard to stay awake, siesta being her favourite thing. Celeste found it funny that Minnie always fell asleep, calling her sleepy-head Minnie and telling her that a daytime nap is okay sometimes. Oh, the number of times I wished Celeste would take a daytime nap.

A new area meant a new community for us to embrace. I need not have worried as they welcomed us. Minnie soon became the star of the shopping centre, with myself becoming known as the lady with the child and Greyhound assistance dog. This was no different to Ipswich but it happened so quickly. I clearly remember the time I was paying for items at the self checkout at Kmart and the lady who was supervising the checkouts came over, calling Minnie by her name. I had never seen this woman before and we had only visited Kmart once previously, having lived in the area for two weeks. I must have looked at her a little bewildered as she then began to explain that she had heard all about Minnie, that the whole staff-room was talking about Minnie. Apparently the staff member at the door when I last visited had stopped to chat with me hence learning Minnie's name. She had then proceeded to tell all the staff of the beautiful Greyhound named Minnie who was doing a fine job as an assistance dog. Everyone was keeping an eye out for her, eager to meet her. She was placing smiles on faces, giving others something to look forward to. Still today every time we go to Kmart the staff say hello to Minnie. We have a lovely friend at the chemist shop who greets us with warm smiles each time we collect prescriptions. She stops to chat with Celeste and ask her what she is up to today, leaning over the counter to take a glimpse at Minnie and say 'hi'. I remember the day I attended to collect scripts by myself. The first reaction was to ask about Celeste. I smiled as it seems I no longer have an identity of my own, but if my little girl is coping with the world and spreading love then my loss of identity is worth it.

It was not long after moving that I was interviewed by the Gold Coast Bulletin newspaper as they had heard so much about Minnie and were interested in her story. A photographer was on my doorstep the next day for a photo shoot. A beautiful article was published telling of how, since being rescued and trained, Minnie had changed the life of Celeste.

It was also at about this time that I was once again contacted by WIN News Sunshine Coast asking for a follow up story on Minnie so off we went for the long drive back to the Sunshine Coast where we met Patricia and the reporter for some more filming. This focussed on the progress of Minnie and the, now published, children's picture book, 'Magical Minnie'.

Moving to the Gold Coast opened up a whole new lot of opportunities for Celeste. We were surrounded by beaches, parks and tourist attractions. Going out, something we never did, soon became something we did every weekend. Celeste was being pushed to her limit; meltdown after meltdown occurred but we soldiered on. Todd McKenney was in town and we were off to say 'hi' again, this time closer to home.

Todd was performing his show 'Todd McKenney Sings Peter Allen' at Twin Towns Club and Resort, Tweed Heads, only a short drive from our house. With Celeste loving music and myself already owning a copy of the album 'Todd McKenney Sings Peter Allen', this was a great opportunity to touch base with Todd and continue broadening Celeste's stage performance experience. Prior to the show we grabbed a moment of Todd's time giving him another Minnie cuddle and Celeste a chance to say hello. Once again there were the ups and downs during the show with Celeste battling the noise and anxiety. One of the issues we had at Twin Towns, which we did not have when attending the Queensland Performing Arts Centre was the fact that the noise caused the floor to vibrate. This vibrated through the chairs slightly but since it was not as bad as the floor I encouraged Celeste to sit on my lap with her feet off the ground. Minnie sat at my feet but with Celeste on my lap this meant she could not cuddle Minnie. This caused a level of anxiety as she wanted to lie on the floor in the dark with Minnie. She was up and down. Down on the floor for a few minutes with head buried then up on my lap with ears covered and humming to herself. She was torn between fear brought on by anxiety and wanting to watch the show. Knowing she needed to hide I eventually took off my jacket and threw it over her head while she sat on my lap. She could peek through the jacket to watch the show but still feel secure from the noise and vibration. Minnie took it all in her stride, helping when she had to but sleeping in between. The vibration of the floor was of no concern to her. By intermission Celeste was finally starting to relax and enjoy the performance. The last part of the show had her smiling and dancing, a little too late as usual but we had the CD at home to dance to the following day.

Moving to the Gold Coast meant we lost our therapy services along with Dr Shah and Dr Chambers who, I still miss today. Both doctors will forever remain in my memory as the two men who led the way to a bright future for Celeste. Minnie then took over and continues the journey. I clearly remember the first time Dr Chambers saw Celeste after we had acquired Minnie. It had been some months since we had seen him as we were in between assessments and mental health plans. Upon entering his office he was full of questions about how assistance dogs work for Autism and the training process of Minnie. As I was leaving he commented on how much Celeste had changed and that he could see by her behaviour this visit, compared to other visits, that Minnie had made an amazing difference. I left the office with a grin from ear to ear. If he had noticed it so early, then surely things would only get better and better.

Having to find a doctor and therapist on the Gold Coast who understood Autism and who Celeste was comfortable with soon became a challenge, one I would have to say has yet to be achieved to the extent that I am confident she is under the best of care. It has always amazed me that where you live within Australia can make a huge difference to what services you can access and the quality of the services. When it comes to services, I have also found that the doctor you see can make or break the success of obtaining what you need. Some doctors have no idea, or just could not be bothered, whereas others are there to help quickly with all the resources available. Cost is also a factor from one place to another, something that in my eyes is unfair as all children should be entitled to the best of therapy regardless of the parents financial situation. Families should not have to choose where they live based on the therapy that is available for their child.

With the move we also left swimming lessons behind. It took us twelve months to find another swim school that understood Autism and anxiety. During that twelve month period Celeste and Minnie visited local lakes and beaches as it was important that Celeste's water confidence was kept at a level where she would enter the water confidently. On the first occasion, three months had lapsed since she had been in a pool. We took her to Shane's father's for a swim in his pool to find that her anxiety about swimming was back and her skills had declined. She stood at the side of the pool wanting to get in but having an anxiety attack about it. She beat herself up and the repetitive self talk started as she rocked back and forth. She kept telling herself she could get in but then hated herself because she was frozen on the spot next to the pool. Minnie and I were also not allowed to move. Every time we took the slightest step away from beside her she would scream, telling us not to leave her. Eventually I encouraged her to let me take Minnie to the very edge of the pool as Minnie wanted to have a look. Minnie peeked into the water and returned to Celeste's side, telling her it was okay and that it looked nice and cool. With the encouragement of Minnie leaning on her we all progressed closer to the edge of the pool, until eventually Minnie got in on the top step and Celeste stood beside her. With Minnie by her side and listening to Celeste's words of self encouragement, Celeste was able to progress to the next step and then to propelling herself across the pool behind her boogey board. Minnie sat in the shallow water on the top step very patiently until Celeste was happy for me to get her out and dry her off. Minnie loves the water, with the lake at the dog park being a favourite spot, so she is always by Celeste's side when getting in the water seems daunting.

Another trip to visit my mum was organised. This would be the first trip for Shane to Nabiac and the first long trip he had taken with Celeste. This trip was to allow Shane and myself some much needed time together. We would spend one night at Mum's and then depart for a one night stay, and much needed adult time, in Forster. Celeste would stay with Nanna. She had never stayed at my mum's, or any house without me but I felt that with the help of Minnie and as she was getting older, this was as good a time as any to give it a go. On the occasion of my mum visiting our house, Shane and I had spent the night at a bed and breakfast not far from home. We had left mid morning and returned early the next morning, keeping the time away as short as possible. Celeste had a 'moment' at bedtime but a chat on the phone to me and some words to Minnie asking her to help saw her dozing off for the night. The night was spent feeling secure next to Nanna in a double bed.

The trip from Nabiac to Forster was a short twenty-five minute drive. It was whale watching season so Mum had organised a whale watching tour which we would all attend and then Shane and I would go off together. Due to being on a boat and the possibility of it getting rough I decided that leaving Minnie behind would be the best option. With the extra hands of Mum, if needed, I was sure we would be okay. I need not have worried as Celeste soon became too seasick to be concerned about anything. We had been on the boat no more than five minutes when Celeste became deathly pale, lying herself down on the floor of the boat wanting to vomit. Mum and I took turns to sit with her comforting her. The trip seemed to go on forever. Occasionally the excitement of the whales would grab her and she would stand up and look out the window, but it was always short lived. Not long before the boat was due to turn back for shore, morning tea was on offer. This was one of the worst mistakes I made. As quickly as my coffee went down it came up again and the return trip was spent vomiting. It was only then I realised how ill poor Celeste felt and by this stage we had been on the boat for some hours. As we pulled into shore, a plastic squeaky whale was purchased as a treat for Celeste, or more as an 'I'm sorry' from me for putting the poor kid through such an ordeal. The decision not to take Minnie was probably a good one, although I do wonder if dogs get seasick. Celeste returned home pleased to see Minnie and with a story to tell her. Overall, Celeste coped well that night without me. She slept in a double bed with Nanna and Minnie by her side, just as she had when left at her own home with Nanna.

As our first year on the Gold Coast came to a close, the renewal of Minnie's public access certification also came around. Although we had been through the testing before it is always daunting. Minnie is part of us when we are out and about and as time passes every command I give her and everything I do with her is done on auto pilot. When it is time for recertification I worry that what I am doing may be wrong or that Minnie will slip up just this once. With Claire and Andrea no longer being with Smart Pups, we were allocated another trainer to do the testing. This was a trainer I had never met before and that worried me a little.

On the day of testing I met the trainer at the local shopping centre. This was an advantage as Minnie knew where she was and the environment was also familiar to Celeste. As usual Minnie was a trouper, not missing a beat. The test was the same as the original certification, making sure Minnie's training was still as refined as ever. I felt my shoulders relax when I was told that she was marvellous and that there was no doubt that I had passed as a handler. Celeste was an angel throughout the whole process. Go team Minnie!

# THE FUTURE

So what does the future hold for both Minnie and Celeste. No one really knows but what I can be sure of is that as a team they are unstoppable. They grow stronger and more resilient every day. I strongly believe in the instincts of a mother and my instincts were not wrong when they told me that an assistance dog was what was needed for my daughter. They say everything happens for a reason. I believe Minnie was never meant to race. She was born small and delicate as the canine Gods had plans for her. There was a little girl waiting for magical Minnie. Her place to shine was always with Celeste.

With Minnie by her side Celeste gained confidence and an 'I can do it' self esteem. She is now eager to talk to people, with the subject naturally being her dog Minnie. She is still self centred, not caring if the person she is talking to is interested in her dog or what she has in her hand but Minnie has provided her with a confidence that enables her to speak up and feel important. With Minnie has come the ability to interact with the environment around her. This is not always in an appropriate or socially acceptable manner and is done with the maturity of a child less than her age but she is doing it. The dream I had of my daughter being able to achieve the things her peers achieve comes true with each little step Celeste takes with Minnie.

Life with an assistance dog is not roses. It comes with challenges and you can never go anywhere without being noticed, especially when your dog is a Greyhound, but the inconveniences that arise from time to time are nothing when compared to the change in our lives that Minnie has provided. One thing Minnie has done for me is make me realise how much Celeste rules my life, our family life. For most families with a child who is heading toward early teens, going out is just a matter of jumping in the car and off you go. For our family, and other families with children with special needs, this will never be the case. Going out involves a lot of planning and comes with a lot of considerations. For myself there came a time when I just stopped going out. I realise now that my life became one of fear of the next meltdown, fear of not being accepted, fear of embarrassment and at times fear of being accused of abusing my child when the scream of a meltdown was taken wrongly. With Minnie in our lives this changed. I suppose Minnie verifies the disability. Not only does she support me by helping me handle Celeste when the going gets tough but she signals a special need to those within the community. Autism is the silent disability. To the naked eye it is unseen. Those with a diagnosis of Autism often look normal. Depending on the level of Autism once a child with Autism reaches adulthood they have often learnt the skills to help them cope in some situations, the Autism staying undetected to the average person. They may be seen as a little strange or not quite there. If I had a dollar for every time someone said to me there was nothing wrong with Celeste then I would be rich. It is times like these I want to hand her over to them for a week and see how grey they are at the end of it.

Minnie has not, and cannot, make the Autism go away. Everyday is still full of suddens screams, head banging, strange noises, rocking and and the inability to cope with the sensory world around her. Unfortunately at this current time there is no cure for Autism but maybe one day the code will be cracked. What Minnie has done for Celeste is provide her with support and with a constant companion who she will have as she grows into a young adult. Minnie does not judge, she does not disappoint and she does not need to understand, she just accepts. To know that there is always someone there to cuddle and to listen is important for Celeste. She does not want to be spoken to. She does not want questions. These only add confusion. She does not want cuddles by a human as this invades her space but cuddles from Minnie are on her terms when needed and without conditions. Prior to Minnie coming into our lives Celeste was housebound. Now she is leading a life of exploration and fun, done on a level that she is comfortable with.

Minnie, in a sense, is like Celeste's guide dog. Spacial awareness is one of the issues our beautiful Minnie has been able to help with, guiding Celeste, preventing her from zig-zagging or from running into things. With Celeste standing on the left of Minnie, holding her special handle, Minnie guides Celeste around objects and keeps her walking in a straight line. With Minnie by her side Celeste has a sense of her place in her environment. When Minnie is not with her Celeste must hold my hand, not only for security but for direction.

The future academically for Celeste is looking a little brighter. With the new found confidence and sense of place she has found by having Minnie in her life, Celeste has started to notice words and numbers within her environment. This has given her an awareness of the importance of words and numbers in our lives and although she continues to struggle, with progress being very, very slow, she is starting to want to attempt to write the odd letter or word. Reading has not yet been attempted but with each day a little light of hope shines. She will most likely never catch up to the level of her peers, as mentally this is not possible, but with each small step she achieves her individual personality and abilities shine.

Celeste has dreams and goals. With her love of animals she speaks of being a vet when she grows up and can often be seen bandaging soft animal toys and listening to their heartbeat with her toy stethoscope. As years have passed she has developed a great knowledge of the animal kingdom, big and small, with David Attenborough and Dr Chris Brown being two people she admires greatly. The future for Celeste will definitely be one that is full of pets of all kinds.

For our family our future holds one of continuing to learn about each other, grow as a team, discover life and share a lot of laughter. Together Celeste and I vow to continue our work promoting Greyhounds as pets and the benefits they give to those with special needs.

There will come a time when Minnie will have to retire from her role of assistance dog. Time will only tell whether Celeste will need another companion to help her or whether Minnie will be able to assist her to gain the skills she needs to approach life alone. Eventually we will have to deal with the loss of our companion as the reality of humans outliving dogs is one that is never far from my mind. This will be one of the hardest days of our lives but together, as a family, we will deal with our loss.

The journey of love, the connection between Celeste and Minnie will live on forever, not only as words on these pages but in our memories and hearts. She truly is one magical dog.

Smart Pups Assistance Dogs, launched in 2011, is a dedicated not-for-profit organisation based on the Sunshine Coast in Queensland, Australia. They specialise in providing trained service dogs to assist children with special needs. Their goal is to improve the quality of life of children with Autism and seizure related syndromes through training dogs in 'task specific' skills. Smart Pups reduce stress levels in children and have a profound effect on the day-to-day lives of the child and family. These positive changes continue as the bond and relationship between child and Smart Pup grows over time.

Placed at the age of 12 to 18 months of age, Smart Pups Assistance Dogs are granted public access and become an integral part of the recipient family's life accompanying them on shopping trips, family outings and even holidays. Smart Pups receive no official funding from the government and relies solely on donations, grants and fundraising activities to operate.

Smart Pups is an approved training institution under the Guide, Hearing and Assistance Dog Act 2009. They are dedicated to raising awareness about the valuable role Assistance Dogs play in the lives of children with special needs.

By purchasing this book you have kindly donated $2 to Smart Pups but they could do with more. It costs $25,000 to train one Smart Pup, with the support, training and re-certification of the dog over its working life being given to each family free of charge. With your ongoing support Smart Pups will be able to ease the burden on the day-to-day living of more families.

*Make a donation today by visiting their website* www.smartpups.org.au. *Donations over $2.00 are tax deductible.*

# Greyhounds New Beginnings

**LIFE AFTER THE TRACK**

Greyhounds New Beginnings – Life After The Track (GNB) is a registered not-for-profit charity that rehomes ex-racing Greyhounds that are no longer able to race. GNB have been rehoming Greyhounds since 2012.

The goals of GNB are:

- Finding suitable forever homes for Greyhounds who can no longer race or are unsuitable for racing
- Providing lifetime support to adoptees and foster carers
- Educating the public about the beautiful nature of the breed and dispelling some common myths and preconceptions.

Greyhounds are well suited to all lifestyles including those of busy families and senior citizens. While it may be nice to want a particular colour and gender of Greyhound, GNB prefer to match a dog's personality to your lifestyle and family dynamics, encompassing any other pets.

The volunteers and foster carers at GNB help to prepare the dogs for their forever homes by teaching them how to become a pet dog. The transition from racer to pet takes a little time and patience. Greyhounds need to get used to a variety of new things in the household environment such as the sound of washing machines, kettles, toasters, ceiling fans and they don't understand glass doors and pools.

All Greyhounds are desexed, vaccinated, microchipped and wormed. Adoption fees vary between the ages of hounds.

By purchasing this book you have kindly donated $2 to Greyhounds New Beginnings but they could do with more.

*For further information or to make a donation*
*visit* www.greyhoundsnewbeginnings.org.au. *Browse the internet site to find the Greyhound companion that will change your life.*

# ABOUT THE AUTHOR

Jennifer Althaus has been involved in the writing and marketing of books for many years in her role as a publicist. She is an avid supporter of the self-publishing industry, having helped many authors write, compile and market their work over the past 10 years. Always busy writing with others she finds little time left to publish her own work, with many projects waiting to see the light. 'A Journey of Love' is her first memoir, with 'Magical Minnie' being her first children's picture book. Jennifer writes regular articles for the online independent magazine, The Australia Times. With a love of words and a creative mind she can see no other life than one that is surrounded by reading and writing.

Currently residing on the Gold Coast, Queensland, Jennifer is the mother of three children, two of whom have Autism. While working and writing she home educates her youngest daughter, Celeste. Her passion lies with a life of positivity, dreaming of a world where positivity is the norm and negativity is long forgotten. She follows the motto 'life is learning, learning is life', embracing each day for the opportunities it brings her to grow, not only as individuals, but universally.

Jennifer loves to hear from people, finding the viewpoints and opinions of others liberating and fascinating. In her eyes all things happen for a reason and we are all connected, if only in a very small way.

Email doublecreations@gmail.com
Facebook www.facebook.com/jenniferalthausauthor
Twitter @GoodGabble.
Join Minnie and Celeste on Facebook:
www.facebook.com/smartpupforceleste

# ACKNOWLEDGEMENTS

This page would have to be one of the hardest to write as so many people have touched our lives and contributed to our journey of love. Everyone who crosses your path contributes in one way or another. Without them life would not be an experience.

**To my family** a huge thank you. I love you all dearly. Without you my life would not be what it is. Without your love and support each day I would not be the strong person I am today nor would I make it through each day. You all enrich my life more than I think you realise.

**To my children:** I love you. Over the years you have challenged me, sent me grey and added a few wrinkles, not to mention stretch marks, but you have given me much joy and shown me what unconditional love is all about. Thank you for being you.

**Shane Althaus :** You came into my life when I was struggling, not only to accept my daughter but to accept myself as a mother and a woman. In the beginning we struggled to find each other and to find us as a team, but instead of running you stayed. With each struggle you met the challenge and we became stronger. In our love for each other we found strength. Although you have struggled to understand my children and the world of Autism you have never weakened, moving forward each day. You are my strength. You are my knight in shining armour who protects me and helps me heal. When you first came into my life Minnie was reasonable new and this book was an idea in the making, a dream. With each doubt that I could write it you gave me words of encouragement. With each word I wrote you told me how proud you were.

**Joan McNamara (Mum):** Thank you for being there on the end of the phone each and every day. When the going gets tough I can always ring Mum. When I struggle to keep my head afloat as I deal with meltdown after meltdown I can always rely on Mum to have a moment to chat. I can only hope my relationship with my children continues along with the strength of the one I have with you.

**Todd McKenney:** A very huge thank you. I cannot thank you enough. You are the reason Minnie is in our life. Thank you for taking a moment of your time to reach out to a family you did not know and offer your support. Your schedule is tight yet you found time for us….it means so much. Your loving, caring soul is one to be cherished, your friendship is greatly valued.

**Smart Pups:** Thank you to the team of trainers at Smart Pups who continue to work hard placing their assistance dogs in the homes of families. This wonderful team changes lives.

**Claire and Andrea:** Thank you ever so much for the time and effort you put into training Minnie. She is a true credit to both of you. Your support and friendship throughout the training journey was valued.

**Sarah and Buffy (Greyhounds New Beginnings):** Thank you ladies for our wonderful Minnie, with a special thank you to Sarah for taking the time to understand what I was seeking in a dog. Thank you Buffy for your continued support and friendship. Thank you to the Greyhounds New Beginnings family for making us feel welcome when we attend events and for sharing your Greyhound adventures with us.

**Leone Sperling:** Thank you for your wonderful editing skills and advice. One day I hope to achieve writing a novel that speaks with the strength that all of yours do. You are a wonderful teacher and a true inspiration.

**Evan Shapiro:** Thank you for your encouragement, wise words of advice, graphic design and publishing skills. You have made my writing journey, which at times could have been stressful, an enjoyable trip full of laughter and friendship.

**Last but not least Celeste and Minnie:** Without you there would be no book. Through both of you I have witnessed an amazing friendship, one that has touched not only my heart but the hearts of many. Minnie, you truly are magical. You have changed the life of my family in ways I could only have imagined. Celeste, I love you. Your courage and desire to overcome your struggles inspire me. Your sweet, beautiful soul is infectious, your smile heart-warming and your laughter lights up a room. You have your life ahead of you and I have no doubt you are going to shine. Together you and Minnie are going to conquer the world.

# MAGICAL MINNIE

JENNIFER ALTHAUS
ILLUSTRATED BY MUZA ULASOWSKI

*I am special. I have Autism.*

*Minnie is special. She is my magical Greyhound....Minnie is a Smart Pup Assistance Dog.*

*Together we conquer the world.*

*'Magical Minnie' is a book that empowers and educates.*

*For children with Autism the world can be a very scary and lonely place. Within the pages of 'Magical Minnie' is a place where they are understood, welcomed and with a friend.*

*Having a friend or family member with Autism is hard. 'Magical Minnie' opens the door for discussions on the behaviour of Autism and the emotions that underlie it.*

*'Magical Minnie' is a beautiful story of a Greyhound Assistance Dog who offers support, love and companionship to a little girl while helping her understand that we are all different but special in our own way.*

### Available on Amazon and from all good bookstores late August 2017.

*www.facebook.com/MagicalMinnieBook*